M000077214

Joyages
3 Minutes to Emotional Health

Claire Burnett, Brett Newman, Ray White

Download the Joyages App

Three Minutes to Help You Navigate Life's Challenges

We teach people to brush their teeth to avoid cavities. We teach them to exercise for cardiovascular health. But what about our brains?

This book was written as a practical guide to help the reader overcome life's daily challenges, as well as improve in the areas that matter to them. You can download the app to support and add to your learning experience.

Joyages delivers a customized experience designed to empower users to become happier in less than three minutes each day.

You Can Also Find More Tools and Resources At Joyages.Com

Joyages

Claire Burnett, Brett Newman, Ray White

Xilo Media

Dallas, Texas

Copyright @ 2019 by Joyages
All Rights Reserved.

All Rights reserved. No part of this book may be reproduced in any
form by any means without the express permission of the authors.
This includes reprints, excerpts, photocopying, recording, or any
future means of reproducing.

If you would like to do any of the above, please seek permission first
by contacting us at
https://www.joyages.com/
or Info@Joyages.com

Library of Congress Control Number: **2019916070**

ISBN **978-0-578-59225-1**

Edition 1.0

Please support our Friends and Sponsors:

 American Foundation *for* **Suicide Prevention** https://afsp.org

 SAN FRANCISCO **SUICIDE PREVENTION** https://www.sfsuicide.org/

 CENTER *for* **BRAINHEALTH** THE UNIVERSITY OF TEXAS AT DALLAS https://brainhealth.utdallas.edu/

 Mental Health America https://www.mhnational.org/

 **SMU** Simmons School of Education & Human Development https://www.smu.edu/Simmons

 **UTA** University of Texas at Arlington https://uta.edu/

 UNT University of North Texas Professional Leadership Program https://www.unt.edu/

Foreword

"The opposite of happiness is not sadness, it is apathy." Unknown

Why We Want You to Be Sad

There are good intentions that come from every direction in our lives that say we should be happy: Our parents want us to be happy. The media wants us to be happy. Our friends want us to be happy. Our companies want us to be happy, and even the government wants us to be happy.

Unfortunately, being normal human beings, we interpret those good intentions as an expectation that we will never be unhappy. We began to believe that negative emotions are bad and should be avoided.

Very early on in our lives we begin to believe that the goal is happiness and all negative emotions are the opposite of reaching that goal. We start to believe that there's something wrong with being sad, angry, frustrated, or any other emotion aside from happy. But no matter how hard we try, difficult moments and negative feelings will come. We can't stop feeling them, that's what being human is all about. But, when we feel sad, we begin to think there's something wrong with us. We think we're failing at life, and guess what - that makes us even more sad. Now, we're sad because we are sad. Doesn't that sound like an exhausting rabbit hole?

Why Social Media Can Make us Sad

Now that we're sad that we're sad, and we think something might be wrong with us, we often turn to the most readily available comparison tool in the history of the world: social media. We look on social media to see if anyone else feels like us. But what do our friends and everyone else post on social media? Most people post about the exceptional moments in their lives. They post the happy times. They post when they're spending time with friends and family, when they're having fun, and when they're succeeding. And we, unintentionally, begin to compare our behind the scenes moments to their highlight reels which makes us even more sad.

It's Not all Bad Though

The good news is we want you to be sad! It's ok to be sad! It is normal to be sad, and even if you are sad today, we want you to know that you can get back to happy. This book will teach you the habits and skills to help you always get back to happy. The key is to feel your sadness, identify what's making you sad, share your thoughts with a friend, practice habits and skills that help you be happier, and remember that it won't last forever. Be ok being sad. Eventually, you will get back to happy.

Brush Your Brain!

That's not something you hear every day. Most of us brush our teeth at least once per day. It's a habit we've done almost automatically ever since we were kids and our parents told us we didn't want to get cavities. We spend 2 to 3 minutes every day to ensure we have good dental health. So why don't we do the same for our Brain Health?

Why not spend 2 to 3 minutes every day learning how to be happier and more successful. Why not invest a small amount of time every day to be better prepared to deal with whatever challenges we will face in life. That is why we created Joyages.

3 Minute Training for Life's Toughest Moments

Throughout this book we'll teach you habits that will help you get back to happy. We'll train you on how to deal with many of the difficult situations in your life, including sadness, and be able to get back to happy.

Each Joyage takes less than three minutes to read and learn. By investing three minutes per day, you'll learn how to truly experience and enjoy the ups and downs in life and get back to happy.

We Also Want You to Experience Stress

Hopefully by now you're not surprised to learn that we also want you to experience stress.

For years, people have been telling us that the effects of stress can kill us. But what the research really shows is that the effects are determined not by the stress itself, but by how we interpret the stress.

Research shows that stress is not actually bad for you. Stress prepares your body to learn, to bond with other people, and to be resilient when you face new challenges. More importantly, no one lives a life without stress. It is a natural part of our lives, just like breathing and eating. So the key is not to live a life without stress, but to learn how to deal with the stress that is an integral part of our lives.

Our goal is not to help you eliminate stress from your life, but to help you learn to accept stress, manage it, then harness the stress to grow and improve. The Joyages we introduce in this book, will help you learn how to do exactly that. There's even an entire section dedicated to teaching you how to deal with stress and make it a positive in your life. Imagine learning how to turn your "killer" stress into a key to your success and happiness. And the best part: you can do this in just three minutes a day!

Use the Joyages App as You Read the Book

Along with writing this book we've also created the Joyages app. Each Joyage you read can be found in video format in the app. You'll also have access to guided Journaling, Quizzes and Assessments, Habit Trackers, and other tools to help your grow and develop with an investment of less than 3 minutes per day.

Joyages includes courses that walk you through growth and development in your relationships, stress, gratitude, career, and overall personal development. Joyages also includes an on-demand Help section where you can access any resources you might need to help you be happy and successful.

You can download the app from the Apple or Android app stores. Just search for Joyages!

How to Get the Most out of Joyages: 3 Minutes to Help with Life's Challenges

We've written Joyages to be quickly consumable in just a few minutes each day. Hopefully it will take you less than 3 minutes to read each Joyage, but you're welcome to spend more time thinking about and practicing the habits we recommend.

Every Joyage includes a tip for how to implement it in your life. Don't try to implement every idea at once. Pick your favorite and focus on that one habit for a month. Then next month, pick another habit to work on. We also recommend sharing what you learn. Real change happens when you learn, practice, and share. Use the Joyages app to track new habits and journal about your experiences.

We've got your back. If you have any questions or suggestions, please reach out to us at info@Joyages.com

We believe that 3 minutes of prevention on a daily basis will help you prepare for and even avoid many of the challenges you will face in life. Invest in yourself and your happiness every day. We believe you're worth it and you deserve a happy and successful life.

Happy Cruising!

To my wonderful wife Lindsey, the past 30 years has been an amazing Joyage!

To my three wonderful kids, Andrew, Spencer, and Gabriele. Everything I do is for you.

A special shout out to all the Highams who have always been there for us.

Thank you from the bottom of my heart to all the believers. With your help, we can change the world and help people live the fulfilled and contented lives they want to live. Special thanks to Wally Gomaa, Joel Dollar, Wayne Irwin, Steve Sanders, Bryan Kanthack, Natalie Adams, Chris and Solomon Thomas, and most importantly my two co-founders Brett and Claire.

-Ray White

Thank you to my wife, Lauren, who first introduced me to why mental health is so important for all of us. You teach me so much every day.

To Luna – You've taught me more about joy than anyone else I know.

And to my parents, for instilling a hunger to be the best person I can be; but also a comfort knowing that it doesn't matter at the end of the day.

- Brett Newman

To Denise & Maddox Burnett: Thanks for teaching me what "through thick and thin" means.

To my Joyages Team (Ray White & Brett Newman): Thank you for always pushing me to be my best self.

To YOU, the reader: Thanks for trusting us with your time!

- Claire Burnett

Contents

Chapter 1: Redefining Happiness

"Most folks are about as happy as they make up their minds to be." --
Abraham Lincoln

"Happiness is not a state to arrive at, but a manner of traveling." – *Margaret
Lee Runbeck*

What You Will Learn in This Chapter:

1. What Happiness Is, And What It Isn't.
2. How to Feel Negative Emotions Without Acting on Them.
3. How to Focus on What Will Truly Make You Happy.

Introduction to Redefining Happiness

"You cannot protect yourself from sadness without protecting yourself from happiness." – Jonathan Safran Foer

Society often sends us the message that we are supposed to be happy and any emotion other than happy is bad for us. But that is not true. In order to find real happiness, it is important to have and embrace all of our emotions. We are human and we have different kinds of feelings, many of them negative in nature. By embracing and accepting those feelings, it will actually be easier for us to find happiness.

Being happy includes being unhappy. Happiness is not all cotton candy and rainbows. For most people happiness is contentment, fulfillment, and satisfaction. It is a belief that you can be the "real you" and life will still turn out great. But for life to be great we must experience all of our emotions and persevere through the ups and downs. We should be authentic in who we are and how we feel: Bad things happen and we feel sad. We see injustices that make us angry. We can be frustrated, scared, or disgusted. Ultimately, a happy person embraces and experiences all of these emotions and other authentic feelings.

Happiness doesn't mean they don't exist, only that you don't dwell on them or become lost in them. Being authentic means experiencing our emotions with an internal understanding that "This too shall pass" and that in the long run, we will find happiness and joy in our lives. So don't worry if you are not constantly happy. Be open and experience all of your emotions in life. Find joy in just being you and remaining confident that happiness can always be a part of your life even while the other emotions come and go as part of your daily life.

Live and feel and be the "real you" and you will be happier.

Activity:
Think about what contentment, fulfillment and satisfaction look like to you.

Joyage #1: Dealing with Our Emotions

"The day we accept we have chosen to choose our choices is the day we cast off the shackles of victim hood and are set free to pursue the lives we were born to live" –Matthew Kelly

Being happy does not mean you do not experience negative emotions. It just means that you don't let those emotions ruin your day or control your life. Feel the emotions. Embrace those negative experiences, and then choose to move forward and find something to be happy about. You can feel negative emotions without having to act on them. Many of us believe that if we are angry, we have to yell or scream. Releasing those emotions is just a part of having those emotions, but the two are separate. You can feel an emotion, and then you can choose how to act on it.

Stephen Covey, in his book, *The 8th Habit*, refers to "the millisecond between action and reaction." If someone cuts you off in traffic, is rude to you, or consciously disappoints you, certain feelings are automatically triggered. There is a small window of time, between the feelings being triggered and your physical reaction, when you get to own your life and decide how you will react. You get to decide whether those emotions will take control and result in a reaction you might regret, or instead, a reaction that is in control and helps you experience and then move on from those feelings. It is not about controlling what you feel; it is about controlling how you react to what you feel.

In the millisecond between action and reaction, you control your life. When something happens to you, you have the option to choose what your reaction will be. Positive reactions will make your life and the lives of those around you happier, while negative reactions can have a negative influence on your happiness and the happiness of those around you.

Between stimulus and response there is a space.
In that space lies our freedom and power to choose our response.
In those choices lie our growth and our happiness.
Stephen Covey, The 8th Habit

Activity:

Write down something that typically makes you angry, like when someone cuts you off on the road, or when someone shows up late to a meeting. Write about how this scenario typically makes you feel, and then write what you can do or think about to choose a reaction you control that will make your life better instead of worse.

Joyage #2: What Doesn't Make Us Happy

"Happiness is more than a mere pleasurable sensation. It is a deep sense of serenity and fulfillment." –Mathieu Ricard

Has the following ever happened to you? You get fixated on the one missing thing in your life that if only you could get it, you'd finally be totally and completely happy? It doesn't matter whether it's the dream job, a fancy car or going on a date with that cute barista who makes the latte hearts.

But when you do get that something, after an initial period of joy, you aren't happier than before you got it. That's called hedonic adaptation or the hedonic treadmill.

Not that kind of treadmill. Though as you'll learn, exercise is an intentional activity that promotes long term health and well-being and probably would increase your happiness, but that's for another Joyage.

When we have a pleasurable experience, neuro-transmitters like dopamine are released in the brain, making us want more of that feeling. We instinctively look for ways to repeat and increase that level of pleasure. We are programmed to want more rather than to be grateful and satisfied with what we have.

In fact, a famous study was done in the 1978 to test this theory. If you had to guess, who do you think said they were happier: recent lottery winners or paraplegics? Unless you've heard of this study, or know a leading question when you hear one, you probably picked the lottery winner. But just a short time after the life-changing event, paraplegics reported higher levels of happiness.

The lottery winners quickly adapted to their material gains. The paraplegics adapted as well, which speaks to the miraculous human ability to persevere that's hardwired into us. But the key difference is that the paraplegics had also hit rock bottom. Every day brought a new challenge, and overcoming each challenge brought joy and confidence that built on itself.

Another reason the lottery winners were less happy is that they didn't earn it. A study at Emory University measured brain activity when subjects had to complete tasks to earn money versus just being given envelopes of money with no effort required. The subjects who worked for their money showed significantly more activity in the pleasure centers of the brain, and these effects lasted much longer than those in the subjects who received money without effort.

So, if we thought money would make us happy, but now we know it doesn't, what do we do? The answer: Rather than focusing on external things like money and fancy cars, focus on what makes us feel good on the inside. Helping another person or working hard to achieve a goal will help us be happier and less stressed. Also spending time with friends and family or just finding something in our lives to be grateful for. Focusing on how you feel on the inside rather than what you can collect on the outside will significantly reduce your levels of stress while helping you be happier and more successful.

Activity:
Make a list of 10 non-material items you are grateful for, like a family member, or being able to spend time with friends.

Joyage #3: Capture the Happy Moments

"Happiness isn't something you experience; it's something you remember."
– Oscar Levent

We are often so busy getting to work or school, getting the next assignment done, or checking items off our "To Do" list that we forget to pause and enjoy the moment. Our life will not suddenly one day become happy. Our lives are made up of years. Our years are made up of days and our days are made up of moments. How we spend the collection of those moments will determine how we spend our lives.

Pause and enjoy a beautiful sky or the smile of a friend. Appreciate a co-worker who helps you out. Stop and think about how lucky you are to have family or friends you can count on. Take a break and enjoy the laughter of children. Linger on the goodbye kiss before you go to work.

Don't fast forward through your life and miss the good parts. Take time to enjoy the moments.

Success Hack:

Don't get so busy working that you forget to appreciate the opportunity to work. Don't get so busy managing that you forget you have the opportunity to manage. Take time to recognize and appreciate the people around you. Balance technology time with people time. Success is not on your phone or your computer texting, answering email or finishing projects. It is in the results of those things and how they affect other people.

Despite what many people think, success is not just a result of working hard, it is a result of seizing opportunities to interact and appreciate other people. It is a result of trying to make lives and the world better. Success comes from the results you produce when you recognize the opportunities to help others. Don't put your head down and focus on work. Lift your head up and look around for opportunities to work hard at helping and appreciating others. Work hard at recognizing opportunities for success. Don't work so hard that you miss your opportunities to be successful.

Activity:
Once each day, pause and appreciate what is going on around you or some small success. Schedule a time daily at work to stand up and talk to or help another co-worker.

Joyage #4: Five Ways to Be Happier

"Because how we spend our days is, of course, how we spend our lives." –
Annie Dillard

We can build happier lives by being happy each day. Here are 5 tips to create a happy day.

1. When you wake up in the morning, think of 3 things you are grateful for.

   Starting the day with gratitude means you are starting off happier and more optimistic. The odds of having a great day go up significantly when you start your day grateful.

2. Practice smiling in the mirror and then share that with 5 people throughout the day.

   Smiling, even fake smiling releases chemicals in your brain that make you happier. Smiling is also contagious, so smiling at someone encourages them to smile and that will be passed on to yet another person. So, start the morning by smiling at yourself and then sharing your smile with others.

3. Nurture a positive relationship during your commute.

   The down time during your commute is a great time to catch up with friends and family. Make it a point to call your mom on Mondays and your brother on Wednesdays. On Fridays, rotate calling friends who live out of town. Texting, emailing, reaching out on social media also works, although not while driving. Share your life and your feelings. Investing in your relationships during your commute will help you be happier and help them be happier.

4. Implement a Random Act of Kindness

    Bring coffee, tape a dollar to a vending machine, or pay for the person in line behind you. Randomly sharing and being kind makes you happier and shares your happiness with others. Who knows, maybe they will pay it forward.

5. Build an autonomy list

    What things in your life do you get to choose? We tend to focus on the things in our life that we don't get to choose, which creates stress. Building a list of things, you can control changes your focus to happier thoughts and helps you feel less stressed.

Activity:
Pick two of the following to do today:
1. Think of 3 things you are grateful for.
2. Practice smiling in the mirror and then share your smile with 5 people throughout the day.
3. Nurture a positive relationship during your commute. For example, call your mom or brother, or text a friend.
4. Implement a Random Act of Kindness. Leave a dollar on the vending machine or pay for the coffee for the person behind you.
5. Build an autonomy list. Make a list of what you can control today.

Closing Thoughts on Redefining Happiness

Hopefully while going through these Joyages, you began to notice a trend. Typically, our definitions of happiness and success became blurred. Happiness is not about money, power or wealth. It's not about increasing the speed at which we believe we need to work so that we could beat our peers in some sort of rate race. The thing is, even your fitbit or apple watch can't measure the stress and intensity this type of thinking comes with.

Since we were young, we've been exposed to the wrong definitions of happiness. And instead of taking everyone else's definitions, we need to define it for ourselves. We need to redefine what success means.

Instead of the size of our homes, let's talk about the size of our heart. Instead of instant gratification, let's focus on gratitude. Let's be human beings instead of human doings.

"Everyone should become rich and famous and do everything they dreamed of, just so they can see that it's not the answer." – Jim Carrey.

What we're searching for is not out there, it's inside. Happiness is an inside job.

How to Implement in Your Life:
1. Recognize that happiness includes all of your emotions. Experience all of your emotions, but don't dwell on them for too long. Acknowledge that "this too shall pass."
2. Choose a positive reaction the next time you experience a negative emotion. Choosing a positive reaction will help you and the others around you be happier.
3. To know what truly makes you happy, think about what makes you happy on the inside rather than what you can collect from the outside. Having an internal focus reduces your stress and makes you feel better.

Pick your favorite concept from this chapter and share with a friend!

Chapter 2: Practicing Gratitude

"Feeling gratitude and not expressing it is like wrapping a present and not giving it." -- William Arthur Ward

What You'll Learn in This Chapter:
1. The benefits of practicing gratitude.
2. Why being grateful is important even when you don't feel like it.
3. How to practice mindfulness to help you choose what's important.

Introduction to Practicing Gratitude

"Silent gratitude isn't very much use to anyone" – Gertrude Stein

The power of gratitude is one of the most common and agreed upon themes in happiness research, and its positive impact is almost universal. Gratitude is also a keystone habit, in that practicing gratitude is foundational and helpful to most of the other habits that improve happiness. Gratitude is geographically universal, as almost every culture has a practice of showing gratitude. In most cases, that includes giving thanks to a higher power or deity.

Grateful people tend to find less conflict and more harmony in their relationships and interactions. They appreciate the action that was taken rather than being upset about the action that wasn't taken.

Feeling grateful has even been shown to help people feel more energized, alert, and enthusiastic.

People who are grateful tend to be more spiritual and more agreeable, likely because grateful people have a deeper sense of belonging.

Did you know that gratitude reduces stress and depression too? Grateful people believe they have more social support, which encourages them to be closer to people and to build harmonious relationships.

The practice of being grateful encourages us to find the positive things in our environment or relationships that are applicable and specific to us. It's a method of thinking positively that connects more to our feelings than to our logic. Grateful people even perform better specifically in areas where they practice gratitude. Sixth- and seventh-grade students who were asked to write what they were thankful for about school showed improvement in their performance at school!

Gratitude also has a pay-it-forward characteristic that creates a virtuous circle. The more grateful we are, the more we want to help other people, which makes us feel better and more grateful. In turn, the people we help become more motivated to help others themselves.

Gratitude does so much to not only make your life better, but to make the lives of those around you better as well. It is a true superpower. So, the next time someone asks you, "which superpower would you wish for?" tell them your superpower is gratitude and share your secret.

"Gratitude is not only the greatest of virtues, but the parent of all the others." --Cicero

Joyage #5: What If I Don't Feel Like It?

"Gratitude isn't bogged down with "what if's" and "when this happens". It is now and it is an enormously powerful force." --Tris Bendickson

Some of you might be thinking; "My life is horrible. I don't really have anything to be grateful for"

Rabbi Noah Weinberg tells a story about a young man who learned how to appreciate life at an early age despite the challenges in his life:

A young man with an unusually happy disposition once came to meet me in Jerusalem. I asked him, "What's your secret?"

He told me, "When I was 11 years old, God gave me a gift of happiness. I was riding my bicycle when a strong gust of wind blew me onto the ground into the path of an oncoming truck. The truck ran over me and cut off my leg.

"As I lay there bleeding, I realized that I might have to live the rest of my life without a leg. How depressing! But then I realized that being depressed won't get my leg back. So, I decided right then and there not to waste my life despairing.

"When my parents arrived at the hospital, they were shocked and grieving. I told them, 'I've already adapted. Now you also have to get used to this.'

"Ever since then, I see my friends getting upset over little things: their bus came late, they got a bad grade on a test, somebody insulted them. But I just enjoy life."

At age 11, this young man attained the clarity that it is a waste of energy to focus on what you are missing, and that the key to happiness is to take pleasure in what you have.

We all have negative aspects to our lives. Life is about having good and bad, ups and downs. Despite what we see on social media, life is full of positive *and* negatives for everyone. But there is always some aspect of our lives where we can find appreciation or hope. Gratitude is not about being thankful for the perfect life, but rather finding something positive we can focus on in our current life.

"We can never really be happy if we can't find a way to be thankful for what we already have." Jacob Sokol

Activity:
Spend 10 minutes counting your blessings. Don't stop writing until the 10 minutes is up. Don't stop until you have over 100 items on your list. Most of us have a lot more to be thankful for than we realize. We take for granted the simple things in our lives, like a bed to sleep on and running water. Be sure to write down even the smallest items.

Joyage #6: Ten Reasons to Choose Gratitude

"Reflect upon your present blessings, of which every man has plenty; not on your past misfortunes of which all men have some." – Charles Dickens

Research has found that participants who recorded their gratitude on a regular basis or participated in other gratitude exercises:

1. Were more successful in attaining their goals
2. Had more energy and were physically healthier
3. Slept better
4. Exercised more
5. Felt more optimistic about their lives and were less stressed
6. Were more alert, enthusiastic, and determined
7. Were more likely to have made progress toward goals
8. Were more likely to help someone else with emotional support or in solving a problem
9. Had more positive moods
10. Felt more connected to others, were less envious, and shared more

That's ten really good reasons to start practicing gratitude right now.

Gratitude doesn't eliminate your negative feelings, but rather it provides you with more reasons to feel positive or enhances your normally positive feelings. Spending time with your friends or family is nice. But taking a few seconds to acknowledge how grateful you are to have those people around you can enhance those feelings and bring them to the surface. When you have a flat tire or car problems, you are likely to feel frustrated or even angry. If you take a second to be grateful that you have a car, and grateful that you know someone who can help, then you will start to have positive feelings that provide a balance to your negative feelings.

Choosing gratitude is not just a good idea, it is a life changing idea. Make it your goal to show more gratitude today.

Activity:
Every morning pause to think about things you are grateful for and write down three of them. Do this daily to create the habit. Longer term, you will want to vary your timing based on how you feel and what works for you. For some people, doing this exercise weekly created more happiness than doing it daily. You can find the timing that works for you.

Joyage #7: How to End the Day on a Good Note

"Gratitude turns what we have into enough." – Aesop

You should choose your ending! We can't remember every moment of every experience, so we selectively remember the highlights and the final parts. A really good experience that ends poorly will be categorized as bad, while a bad experience that ends well will be categorized as good. One year from now we will remember that, in general, the experience was good or bad based on the highlight and our last memory, but we probably won't remember many of the other details. This is mostly an unconscious process, but we can positively influence it by purposely reviewing the good parts at the end of every experience. Don't spend the last hours of your day ruminating about what you did wrong. Instead take the time to review what went right and why it went right. We all have problems and challenges throughout the day, but you can end the day on a positive note that builds on your strengths and gives you reasons to be happy about the day.

On your commute or at night as you sit down on your bed, think through the day and remember the good things that happened that day. A month from now you will remember mostly good days and at the end of the year, you will believe you had a good year. Much of your happiness is based on your memories, not on what actually might have happened. You can choose to focus on the bad memories and have a crummy life or focus on the good memories and have a great life.

There is good and bad in every day. Ask yourself "What was good today?" Go to sleep thinking about what was good, even if it was one small thing.

Activity:
Everyday this month, finish your day by thinking of something good that happened. Write it down in a gratitude journal, in the notes section of your phone, or in the Joyages app!

Closing Thoughts on Practicing Gratitude

"The single greatest thing you can do to change your life today would be to start being grateful for what you have right now. And the more grateful you are, the more you get." – Oprah Winfrey

Gratitude is a happiness superpower because practicing gratitude is one of the easiest and most effective methods for reducing stress, being happier, and becoming more successful.

People who practice gratitude have better relationships, are more energized and alert, have a deeper sense of belonging, and have lower levels of stress and depression.

At the end of every day, review the things you are grateful for rather than the things that went wrong. This one daily practice can make your weeks, years, and life happier, one day at a time.

Other ways to practice gratitude include writing in a gratitude journal, writing letters of gratitude to people in your life, or even finding a gratitude partner to share the great things in your life with someone else.

Our lives are filled with positive and negative moments. We can focus on the negative which will make us less happy and more stressed, or we can choose to focus on the positives in our lives and become less stressed, happier and more successful.

Keep the following in mind to help you practice gratitude:

Practicing gratitude is a great way to decrease stress and depression. By realizing what you're grateful for, you become much more appreciative of what you do have, rather focusing on what you don't have.

Being grateful is about putting what life has given you in a positive light. Even people who have lost limbs practice gratitude in their lives' and are generally happy people. Try to find the silver lining in all that you do.

Chapter 3: Finding Purpose

"We are more fulfilled when we are involved in something bigger than ourselves." – John Glenn

What You Will Learn in This Chapter:

1. What is a higher purpose?
2. The importance of having a higher purpose
3. How to discover your purpose and write out a higher purpose statement.

Introduction to Finding Purpose

"Focusing your life solely on making a buck shows a certain poverty of ambition. It asks too little of yourself. Because it's only when you hitch your wagon to something larger than yourself that you realize your true potential." –Barack Obama

A higher purpose is your reason for getting up every morning. It is something that you are committed to that is bigger than just you. It can be as simple as helping your teammates succeed or as complicated as solving world hunger.

Based on research by the Center for Disease Control, only 21% of adults strongly agree that their life has a clear sense of purpose. In two other studies, 90% of alcoholics and 100% of drug addicts thought their life was meaningless. In several polls spread across several time periods and countries, when people were asked what was very important, "having a purpose or meaning in life" was chosen by 80% to 90% of respondents, while money was chosen by around 16%. Having purpose and meaning in your life has been connected to happiness, life satisfaction, physical health, and self-esteem. Having purpose and meaning can even improve our health at the cellular level, providing us with a better immune system. Purpose and meaning are important in our lives, helping us both emotionally and physically. But unfortunately, many of us never actually have a tangible sense of what purpose or meaning are in our own lives.

Part of happiness is having a higher purpose--something to strive for that is bigger than ourselves. We all want to matter and to make a difference in the world, at work, or in someone else's life. Our higher purpose is how we find deep meaning and fulfillment in our lives.

"Many persons have a wrong idea of what constitutes true happiness. It is not attained through self-gratification, but through fidelity to a worthy purpose." – Helen Keller

Joyage #8: Finding Your "Why" Is Important

"The two most important days in your life are the day you are born and the day you find out why." – Mark Twain

Have you ever had the feeling that something is missing? Everything should be good. You have great relationships and/or a great family, a great job where you are doing well and moving up, and everything in your life seems to be in place. But you can't shake that feeling of "there must be more". In these moments, you need a purpose to help you understand where to go from there. It serves as your answer to the question "Why?"

- Why am I doing these things?
- Why should I get up in the morning?
- Why should I put in this level of effort?

In Greek mythology, King Sisyphus is punished by the gods and forced to roll a boulder up a mountain all day every day, only to watch it roll back down at the end of the day. No matter how hard he works, the rock never stays at the top of the mountain; and his work is pointless. Our lives often fall into the trap of becoming like Sisyphus: We do the same thing every day, but rarely do we see progress.

This Sisyphean pursuit often starts after the honeymoon at our job ends for example. Initially we work to gain something for ourselves, such as buying our first car or our first apartment. Focusing on our own personal gain can be motivating for a while. But once we reach that goal, the reward and internal feeling of satisfaction are fleeting and always seem to be out of reach. We move on to the next bigger goal, often not even stopping to celebrate our accomplishments. After several months, or whatever timeframe it takes to accomplish those first basic goals, we lose excitement and focus, and fall into a routine. Over the years, we settle deeper and deeper into this routine.

Prying ourselves out of that routine requires purpose – something we can work toward that makes us want to get up every day. That usually includes something bigger than ourselves.

Once you understand your "Why," you can get the "what" and the "how" in order. You can take action that will fulfill your passions and feel meaningful in your life. Your "Why" provides clarity for taking that next step.

Dennis Waitley provides an analogy of a suitcase with a million dollars in it. The story explains that all you must do to claim the one million dollars is drive across town and pick up the suitcase in under one hour. You would probably make two decisions: you would start immediately, and you would overcome any obstacle, traffic problem, or even a natural disaster to get to that suitcase in under an hour.

The decisions you would make and the actions you would take are probably very different from what you would do if you were driving across town for a meeting, a doctor's appointment, or some other mundane activity. The one million dollars is a clear and motivational "Why." You can clearly visualize how it will impact your future, and you would push yourself to extreme measures to claim that prize. We can tap into that same motivational current by finding a clear "Why" for our lives. Knowing and understanding our "Why" will help us start early every day and overcome obstacles that would otherwise deter us from our goals. Find your "Why" for everything you do, and you will discover the ability to overcome any obstacle that is thrown in your way.

Activity:
Brainstorm your "Why" - Why do you work? Why do you try to wake up on time? Why do/did you go to school?

Joyage #9: Create Your Higher Purpose

"This is the true joy in life, the being used for a purpose recognized by yourself as a mighty one..." – George Bernard Shaw

Higher purpose comes from being connected to something bigger than yourself. It is about giving rather than receiving. Many people looking for meaning in their lives find it by getting involved in causes greater than themselves, such as family, country, team, company, religion, or anything else they can identify with.

Start by asking, "How can I be of service" or "how can I help someone else?" "How do I help others with the talents, experiences and skills that I have? How can I make the world a better place? How do I plant seeds of greatness in the lives of those around me? How do I make an impact in the circles of influence where I find myself? How does what I do impact people? A video game programmer helps people have fun. A food service worker helps people have a relaxing, enjoyable meal. A school janitor helps create a clean and safe learning environment for children. What are the positive impacts you can have on other people?

Focus on what's inside vs. outside. A paycheck is external motivation. Helping a coworker is an internal motivation. External motivation, such as getting a paycheck or recognition from our peers, is an important part of our lives; however, the key is to make sure that is not the only form of motivation. What makes you feel good inside? What makes you feel peaceful and fulfilled? Helping another person or making an impact on the goals of your company or team provides internal rewards and fulfillment that lasts.

Our higher purpose can also be related to our dreams. We all have dreams of what we want to be or do, but we often ignore them or hide them because they seem impossible or unreasonable. We should uncover them and explore them. Find out how your dreams may be related to other people. Knowing our dreams can help us define what will provide meaning in our lives.

Don't limit your thinking to one higher purpose in only one part of your life. You can have more than one higher purpose, and each can be related to your work, family, religion, hobbies, etc. Creating a great environment for your kids and contributing to team accomplishments at work can both fit into your life. Feel free to experiment with different types of higher purposes in different areas of your life.

"If you can't figure out your purpose, figure out your passion. For your passion will lead you right into your purpose." – Bishop T.D. Jakes

To help you find your higher purpose, identify those times when you feel truly happy. When you are contented rather than excited and thrilled. What are those things you do every week that you are passionate about? What are the things that give you an almost irrational sense that you can't give up. For what types of activities do you say, "I love to do that; it gives me such joy and fulfillment"?

Ok, to pull all of this together, try this activity. Pull out something to type or write on. Now pretend you are 100 years old and explaining to your great-grandchildren what is important in life. What would you tell them about your life? Take 10 minutes and write down the most important things you would want to tell them. Now read through that list and create your statement:

My Higher Purpose Statement:

I {Active Verb} {Who} {Details}

Here are 3 examples to help you get started.

1. I will live and mentor an authentic, adventurous, spiritual life, while being a catalyst for positive change.
2. I will interact with others to improve my home life and obtain pleasure and recognition.
3. I will be a spokesman for wildlife issues and help people connect their daily actions to saving the wildlife on this planet.

Remember, you are looking for your higher purpose and not someone else's. You don't have to impress anyone or get anyone's approval. Your higher purpose doesn't have to be related to your work, and you can have more than one. Most importantly, you can change it if it doesn't feel right or if your circumstances change. Don't stress over it, and don't worry about getting it perfect. Just try something and keep trying until you feel good inside and can smile when you think about it.

Now that you have a higher purpose, create a habit of reading it every day. Memorize it. When you wake up in the morning and you have a hard time getting started, remind yourself of your higher purpose.

Activity:
Try writing your higher purpose statement.

1. Start with "I."
2. Add an active verb that describes what you do or want to do – help, create, design, provide, lift, build, etc.
3. Add the "who." Who specifically fits into your Higher Purpose?
4. Add in any details that help make it unique to you.
5. See if it fits and make changes until you are comfortable.

It can be anything you want it to be, and you can change it at any time. Like a finely tailored suit, it needs to fit you and make you feel proud when you show it to others.

Joyage #10 Purpose Through Spirituality

"Your purpose in life is to find your purpose and give your whole heart and soul to it." – Buddha

If you're looking for your higher purpose, that deeper meaning that gives you the motivation to get out of bed in the morning, a good place to start is with your spiritual beliefs. For some this is through an organized religion, but it doesn't necessarily have to be. Most religions, even those that seem very different on the surface, teach similar concepts when it comes to a higher purpose. They encourage believing in something greater than ourselves and they emphasize the personal growth you can achieve by contributing to the common good.

Whether you believe in God or you simply put your faith in the oneness of the universe, religion and spirituality offer us a way of looking at life that gives us hope for the future and can actually increase our happiness.

Studies show that people who believe in something bigger than themselves live longer. These people report that they have found meaning in their lives and that they are happier than people who don't have spiritual beliefs. The biggest reason for this is that virtually all spiritual belief systems provide an outward focus rather than an inward focus. They emphasize the importance of loving others, giving to others, and doing things for the greater good of society—rather than just living for ourselves.

Not only do you create actual good in the world when you focus outward, but it takes your focus away from any nagging stresses you may have rattling inside your brain, which can decrease the impact of stress hormones like cortisol on your body. So, you can see how focusing outwardly can actually build strength in your body, mind, and spirit!

Even if you weren't raised as a religious or spiritual person, you can start exploring your spirituality and find what resonates with you. See what fits. Then, craft a personal statement of commitment showing how you are going to use your passions, strengths, and skills to impact the world outside yourself that is in keeping with your beliefs.

For example, if you are a mother raising two children, you could say: *I am raising my children with love so that they can be happy, purposed children of God.* Or, you could say, *I am raising my children so they can become happy, loving citizens of the universe.*

You can make statements about your family life, your job, your hobbies, or your work in the community. You can find a spiritual purpose in virtually everything you do, and by doing that, you can start to build more happiness into your life.

Activity:
List 5 ways that you can focus outwardly this week. Like spending extra time with friends, volunteering, or helping a family member in need.

Joyage #11 Declaring Your Purpose

"What you do makes a difference and you have to decide what kind of difference you want to make." – Jane Goodall

Steve Foster, the pitching coach for the Colorado Rockies, recently shared a story of when he was called up to the major leagues by the Cincinnati Reds. They were playing the Montreal Expos. Steve had to meet the team in Canada, but he had never traveled outside of the country. The customs agent asked the standard question: "Why are you here, Mr. Foster?" Steve said, "I'm here to play against the Montreal Expos." The agent didn't look convinced, because Steve was all by himself. Then the agent said, "What do you have to declare?" If you've never gone through customs, that's a normal question about what you are bringing into the country. But Steve had no idea what he meant. Steve said, "Pardon me?" The agent asked again, "What do you have to declare?" Steve said, "Well, I'm proud to be an American." Needless to say, he was actually handcuffed and questioned, making him late to his first major league game.

Whether you travel internationally or not, we all have something to declare. No matter your nationality, you have something to declare. That something is this: I have a purpose in my life.

You were made for a purpose and you are on this planet to discover your purpose and to fulfill it. But it all begins by believing your own words— and believing your own declaration. In fact, it may seem a little strange, but you need to say out loud, "I have a purpose and reason to be alive." Sometimes you have to preach to yourself.

Here are your 3 declarations for the speech you can give yourself today:

Declaration #1—I reject frustration and choose the joy of the journey.

Have you ever had to get up early and as hard as you try, you simply can't fall asleep? You begin to get frustrated and worked up because you can't fall asleep, which makes it harder to sleep! It's only when you relax that you find rest. The same is true in finding your purpose. The more you allow yourself to get frustrated in your search for meaning, the harder it will be to find. Relax and decide you will choose joy in the journey.

Declaration #2—I am here to make a difference.

You aren't on this planet to take up space or to simply occupy an office. Everyone has the opportunity to make a difference in this world. Part of finding your purpose will be to discover what unique difference you can make in this world.

Declaration #3—Part of my purpose is to serve other people.

We sometimes forget that we find real, lasting fulfilment in serving others. You can spend a day working on your project and you will find a level of satisfaction. But spend a day helping a poor family buy some groceries, or work on a house with Habitat for Humanity, or serve in a soup kitchen, you will find a deep-seated happiness in your soul. That is because you are wired to find fulfillment in serving others.

You have a purpose in this life. Don't forget it. So, reject frustration and choose joy. Declare you are here to make a difference, and then search for people you can serve. For it is there, you just might find why you're here.

Activity:
Take each of these declarations and make them your own.

1. For Declaration #1, ask yourself what will make you joyful in your journey.
2. For Declaration #2, ask yourself what difference you want to make, then start on a plan of how you will make that difference.
3. Lastly, for Declaration #3, think of ways you can serve other people, whether that be at work, with your friends, or with your family.

Pick one way you can help others and follow through.

Closing Thoughts on Finding Purpose

"Live in the present. Launch yourself in every wave, find eternity in each moment..." – Thoreau

Do you feel like you're always waiting on the next thing to happen? Whether it's the next milestone, or the next holiday, or the next promotion—there just seems to sometimes be a lack of contentment in your life and a frustration if you're not completely "living your purpose." It's the "are we there, yet?" question we all asked our parents on family road trips. In fact, sometimes, you can become so frustrated about not knowing your purpose in life, that you find yourself missing what is happening today.

Read this poem by Robert Hastings. It's called The Station and it's a reminder that the joy of life is the journey and not the destination.

We see ourselves on a long trip by train that spans the continent. We look at the life that passes us by as our train moves down the track. But uppermost in our minds is the final destination. On a certain day at a certain hour we will pull into the station. Bands will be playing and flags waving. Once we get there so many wonderful dreams will come true and the pieces of our lives will fit together like a completed jigsaw puzzle. How restlessly we pace the aisles – waiting, waiting, waiting for the station. "When we reach the station, that will be it!" we cry. "When I'm 18." "When I buy my new SL Mercedes Benz!" "When I put the last kid through college." "When I have paid off the mortgage!" "When I get a promotion." "When I reach the age of retirement, I shall live happily after that!" Sooner or later we must realize there is no station, no place to arrive at once and for all. The true joy of life is the trip. The station is only a dream. It constantly outdistances us...

So, stop pacing the aisles and counting the miles. Instead, climb more mountains, eat more ice cream, go barefoot more often, swim more rivers, watch more sunsets, laugh more, cry less. Life must be lived as we go along. The station will come soon enough.

Contentment is found in enjoying life one day at a time. Purpose is found on the journey and is not the destination.

Today is all you have. Today is all you need. Today is all you can handle. Enjoy life today. The journey is shorter than we all think.

How to Implement in Your Life:

Your higher purpose is what makes you get out of bed in the morning. It gives your life meaning and a goal to work toward every day.

By having a "why" or a higher purpose, it influences how you do your day to day tasks. Knowing and understanding our "why" will help us start early every day and overcome obstacles that would otherwise deter us from our goals.

Think of multiple areas in your life that you want to impact to create several higher purposes in your life. Think of your why and who you want to impact, and take a few moments to write your higher purpose statement. Live with it, practice it, and change it. It is yours. It doesn't have to be perfect, it just needs to help you understand and focus on your "why" each morning.

Special thanks to Dr. Brent Taylor for his contributions to these and other Joyages.

Chapter 4: Overcoming Stress and Anxiety

"Worry does not empty tomorrow of its sorrow; it empties today of its strength." – Corrie Ten Boom

What You Will Learn in This Chapter:

1. What stress is and how to change it from a negative to a positive motivator.
2. How to reduce stress and respond appropriately to your stress triggers.
3. Methods to manage the stress in your life.

Introduction to Overcoming Stress and Anxiety

"It's not the load that breaks you down, it's the way you carry it." – Lou Holz

For most of us, the term stress is associated with negative connotations. We think of stress as a bad thing that we want to eliminate from our lives. This feeling is magnified by the research and hundreds of articles showing that prolonged, continuous stress exacerbates symptoms related to many common causes of death.

But the truth is, stress is actually good for us and has evolved to help us respond, grow, change, and even survive. Stress prepares us for challenges, saves us from dangers, and motivates us to make changes in our lives that are good for our long-term survival and flourishing.

This concept is important: Stress is not bad; it prepares and motivates us. It is how we choose to respond to stress that can result in negative consequences. We can get caught in the negative 'stress is bad' spiral or we can choose to manage and adapt to stress.

In this Joyage we will teach you how to change stress from a negative in your life to a positive motivator. You will begin to recognize when stress in preparing you for success or motivating you toward personal growth. We will talk about what stress is, how to recognize your triggers, and several methods for managing the stress in your life.

Joyage #12: What Is Stress?

"You can't always control what goes on outside, but you can always control what goes on inside." – Wayne Dyer

Stress is our body's natural reaction to an outside stimulus or changes in our environment. It is something that everyone experiences on a regular basis. Since it is almost impossible to eliminate stress from our lives – even during a vacation you will experience stress, we need to learn how to manage our responses to stress.

When you feel stress, it is a result of your body releasing hormones like Cortisol and Adrenaline. These hormones are preparing your body to react to a threat, so they increase your heart rate and breathing, make your senses sharper, and send more oxygen to your muscles. This redirecting of resources also slows your logical thought processes so you can focus on the perceived threat.

This is all part of your "Fight or Flight" responses and is your body's way of preparing you to escape or face the threat. The "Fight or Flight" response helped our ancestors survive because they were able to either run away or turn and fight as the sabre tooth tiger appeared. Thankfully in today's modern world, we don't run into sabre tooth tigers very often, but we still have that automatic stress response. There is also a slower version of the "Fight or Flight" response that happens over days or weeks. A sabre tooth tiger is an immediate threat, but we have also evolved to recognize that winter is coming and to feel a constant and ongoing stress about preparing our food and shelter or moving to a warmer client. This stress helped motivate us to change or move as our environment changed.

The bad news is our instincts can't tell what is truly life threatening and what is just a little worrisome, so we often have life or death stress reactions to more mundane, everyday challenges.

The good news is that after the initial reaction we have complete control of our stress, and we can actually use the stress in a positive way and find ways to manage or reduce our stress.

Activity:
Take the time today to start identifying what your stressors are and why.

Joyage #13: How to Win the Stress Battle Between Your Two Brains

"The greatest weapon against stress is our ability to choose one thought over another." – William James

Stress is a battle between two parts of our brain, the reptilian or instinctual part which is trying to save our lives, and the thinking brain which thinks through and solves problems. The reptilian brain thinks we are going to die, so it sends chemical signals to prepare us to take action that will save our lives. It literally bypasses our thinking brain because it doesn't want us to waste time thinking through the problem. As the thinking brain catches up and starts to think, it's first reaction is, "I just got a signal that there is danger and I might die, what should I do?" The stress gets better or worse for us based on how we decide to handle our thoughts related to those signals.

One of the challenges with interpreting and thinking through these stress signals is that they made more sense during prehistoric days when everything was a danger and when we were constantly at risk for death from sabre tooth tigers, a changing environment, or other short term and long-term threats. In today's modern world we rarely run into life threatening situations. Unfortunately, our reptile brain doesn't realize that. It sends stress signals based on the threat of death, even if the stress is related to just meeting someone new. In fact, one of the most common stress inducing stimuli is the fear of social rejection. In prehistoric time we only survived if we stayed with our group for protection. So, when we are meeting new people, giving presentations, or delivering on a project, our reptilian brain interprets possible death from social rejection and sends stress signals that say "take action" or you might die.

Unfortunately, for most of us, the signals are not that clear. Although we are only giving a presentation, we subconsciously have a sense that we might die. When the thinking brain kicks in, it's first thought is something is very wrong, and I need to act. Our natural habit is to amplify that thought and start worrying about all the bad things that might happen. Every time we worry about a minor negative scenario, for example, someone not liking us, our reptilian brains is screaming "social rejection means death" and sending more stress chemicals which causes us to worry more. We create a negative cycle that can lead to chronic stress, anxiety, or worse. It is actually our continued negative reaction to the stress that can kill us rather than the original stimulus of meeting someone new.

Now the good news. This is the point where we can take control of our stress. The chemicals released by the reptile brain tell us something is very wrong and subconsciously we even think we might die. As our thinking brain becomes active, we can make a choice to either negatively encourage those unclear feelings of danger or we can choose to recognize what is happening, take control, and take actions to reduce our stress which will help us feel safer and calmer.

Once we recognize these feelings of discomfort as stress, we can begin to identify the triggers and what is causing the stress. Then we can logically think through what actions we can take to feel like we are back in control.

For example, if you were meeting someone new and your reptilian brain is sending signals that you might die because of social rejection, your thinking brain can then intervene and recognize, "I started feeling uncomfortable when I was about to meet someone new. I know I will survive even if they don't like me. This feeling can remind me to look them in the eyes, repeat their name and listen carefully to what they say." Your thinking brain can choose a positive response to the stress and actually use the stress to help you prepare for a better introduction.

Remember, stress exists to prepare us and to motivate us. We can focus on and create a negative cycle by ruminating or constantly worrying on the stress, or we can use our thinking brain to recognize the trigger and determine how we can be prepared and motivated to do better. The bottom line is we get to choose.

Activity:
Think about one common thing that often stresses you out. It could be meeting new people or having too much to do at work. Then, think of what actions you can take to be back in control. You can remind yourself that you won't die when meeting someone new or remember to prioritize your tasks at work to accomplish what's most important.

Joyage #14: Recognizing Your Stress Triggers

"When I look back all these worries, I remember the story of the old man who said on his deathbed that he had had a lot of trouble in his life, most of which had never happened." – Winston Churchill

A quick recap on stress: Our reptile brain interprets triggers, for example the thought of meeting new people or making presentations, as social rejection that could lead to death, so it sends chemicals to help us be prepared and motivated. Our thinking brain eventually catches up and we get to choose whether to maintain the cycle of negative life-threatening thoughts or to take control and take action that will calm our fears and reduce our stress.

So, let's start by identifying our triggers and the associated negative stress inducing thought patterns. Remember our thoughts are very non-threatening, but our reptile brain reacts and sends chemicals because all it understands is that "we might die."

Below are a list of modern triggers and the related concept the reptile brain thinks "I might die" from:

1. Not enough money - A lack of food or shelter
2. Meeting new people - Social rejection because I am not allowed in the group
3. Making a presentation - Social rejection because they don't agree with my ideas or don't think I am capable
4. Not delivering on a project - Social rejection for not fulfilling my role in the group
5. Being Late - Social rejection from missing out or not meeting the standards of the group
6. World Problems - A different environment that I cannot adapt to
7. Family Interaction - Social rejection from my key protection group

The first step to reducing stress is recognizing these triggers and understanding why they feel so much worse than reality. Our brain can create worse scenarios as it tries to explain why the reptile brain thinks it might die. So, identify the trigger and decide what action you are going to take to reduce the stress. How are you going to leverage the chemicals that are there to help you be prepared and motivated?

Activity:
Now pause and make list of what you think triggers stress in your life. Put in notes on your phone and you can always add to it the next time you feel stress.

Joyage #15: How to Manage Your Stress

"You are braver than you believe, and stronger than you seem, and smarter than you think." --.Christopher Robin

When we start managing stress, the first thing to recognize is that you are in control. You can control the amount of stress you experience based on how you respond to your stress triggers.

If a friend jumps out from behind a door and startles you, your initial jump or scream is a very natural reaction. It is your body preparing to save you from a life-threatening situation. But once your brain catches up and recognizes that this is a friend and not a threat, your fear and chemical reactions in your body quickly fade away. This is you managing your stress. Once you realize it is possible, you can manage other forms of stress in the same way.

The most common form of stress management is relaxation techniques. These might include meditation, focusing on a word, counting techniques, tranquil visualization, yoga, or deep breathing exercises. Pick the ones that most interest you and practice them regularly. For this video let's focus on deep breathing exercises

These are relatively easy to practice and implement and can be done anywhere at any time. When you first notice signs of stress, acknowledge the stress and take a long, deep breath counting to four before you stop. Count one one-thousand, two one-thousand, three one-thousand, four one-thousand. Hold your breath for a count of four and then finally, let your breath out slowly on another four count. Repeat four times in a row and then check your level of stress. If it is still high, then complete the deep breathing cycle another four times or until you feel your body start to relax.

Now that your body is relaxed and you are thinking clearly, determine how you are going to use the stress signal to prepare you or motivate you to be better.

Activity:
Try practicing meditation for 7 days straight and then track how it made you feel.

Joyage #16: Three Ideas to Help You Deal with Stress & Anxiety

"It's not the stress that kills us, it is our reaction to it." – Hans Selye

Stress is not bad; it prepares and motivates us. It is how we choose to respond to stress that can result in negative consequences. We can get caught in the negative 'stress is bad' spiral or we can choose to manage and adapt to stress. Here are 3 ways to help you deal with stress.

1. *Relaxation Techniques* - Stress puts your body on high alert. It sends chemicals that cause your heart rate and breathing to increase and your muscles to tense. Learning to relax and reverse these changes is one of the most important techniques for combating the negative effects of stress.

   - **Meditation** - learn how to focus your mind on peace and tranquility, to the exclusion of all other outward distractions.
   - **Counting** - Count to ten slowly. If you don't feel relaxed at ten, keep counting. Think about the numbers as you count.
   - Try taking a **Yoga** class on a regular basis. Yoga teaches many of these types relaxation techniques and research shows yoga can be a great stress reliever.
   - **Deep Breathing** - Breathe-in, hold your breath, and then breathe out, each for a slow count of four. This is a simple relaxation technique that you can do anywhere at any time.

2. *Exercise* - Exercising on a regular basis releases stress fighting chemicals and helps you reduce stress even when you don't know you are stressed. It can be as simple as taking a walk, going for a swim, lifting weights, or joining some form of exercise class.

3. *Sharing with Friends* - Stress dissipates more quickly if you can spend a few minutes sharing your feelings with friends. Even hearing their challenges can help you feel calmer and less stressed. Spending time with friends helps you relax quicker and gives you other things to think about, besides your most recent stress trigger.

You get to choose how you respond to stress. The next time you start feeling stress, pause and choose.

Activity:
Pick one of these 3 ideas, Relaxation, Exercise, or Sharing with Friends or see our other videos with even more ideas on how to respond to stress.

Joyage #17: How Helping Works

"We must give more in order to get more. It is the generous giving of ourselves that produces the generous harvest." – Orison Swett Marden

Being kind to others reduces our stress and makes us happier, since helping people requires you to see them in a positive light. If you reach out to help people rather than avoid them, you must make the transition in your mind from judgment and fear to empathy and compassion. It also creates a reciprocal reaction in them, like a smile or gratitude, which then makes you happier and less stressed. That cycle continues as they then move to the next person, still thinking positively about you, and share a smile with someone new.

Imagine a woman in business attire walking towards the same building as you. She has a sour or put-out look on her face. Your initial thoughts might be that she is mean or angry and you should avoid her. But a thought flashes through your mind: what if she has had a bad morning, or what if she is concentrating on what she needs to get done at work today? So, you open the door for her. She looks up, at first confused, and then recognizes the kindness you are offering. Her look changes from sour to a smile as her mind clicks away from whatever was bothering her to appreciation of this small gesture. Her smile makes you smile, and you are both likely to carry that smile into the elevator and the office. This doesn't work every time; but you will become happier as you find new ways to be thoughtful and kind to people, whether they reward you with a smile or not. Practice assuming positive intent in all people for an allotted time block, say 2 hours in the morning when your brain is still firing on all cylinders.

Helping others gives us the opportunity to use our strengths and interests. Cooking for others or helping to build a house with Habitat for Humanity are great examples. Helping others also serves as reinforcement that we are good people. We all like to think that we are, but helping others is the concrete proof that we should feel good about who we are. It connects us to people in ways we might not expect, as we get to be surprised by other people's positive reactions to what we are doing. Helping others helps us find a sense of meaning and see how fortunate we are to have what we have.

Stress and sadness distract us from others and the small moments we have to offer help. If you are feeling sad or stressed, don't miss the moments. That is the best time to pause and help someone else, since it will make them feel better and that in turn will help you feel better.

You can create a virtuous circle of stress reduction and happiness for you and others just by making small gestures of kindness and help. Try it today.

Activity:
Brainstorm a few ways that you can help others this month. Possibly bring coffee to the office, or schedule time to volunteer at your local homeless shelter. Then, follow through with your plans.

Joyage #18: Simple Ideas for Helping Others

"...Doing a kindness produces the single most reliable momentary increase in well-being of any exercise we have tested." –' Martin Seligman

So how do you get started helping others?

1. Perform 1 Random Act of Kindness per day from the list below or come up with your own.
    a. Tape money to a vending machine
    b. Help someone in need cross the street
    c. Open a door for someone
    d. Buy a friend a drink or a coffee
    e. Help a friend through a stressful time
    f. Bring donuts to the office

2. Find a charity or cause that matches your values. Find ways to help, even if it is for only a few hours each month. Share the opportunity with your team members at work.

3. Set a daily reminder on your phone to do something nice for someone.

Closing Thoughts on Overcoming Stress

Stress is not bad; it prepares and motivates us. Rather it is how we choose to *respond* to stress that can result in the negative consequences we so often associate with stress. We can get caught in the negative 'stress is bad' spiral or we can choose to manage and adapt to stress.

Stress is our body's natural reaction to an outside stimulus or change in our environment. It is something that everyone experiences on a regular basis. There is no life without stress.

Stress has an impact because one part of the brain is sending signals that we might die. It is up to our "Thinking Brain" to counteract and calm those feelings so we can make good decisions about how we want to respond to the stress triggers.

To manage and reduce our stress we need to identify the triggers and determine our response to those triggers. We choose different responses depending on the trigger. For example, if we are stressed about meeting new people, we can remind ourselves that they are probably a little nervous as well. If we are stressed about money, we can work on a budget so we feel more in control, and if we are stressed about making a presentation, we can use deep breathing techniques and turn the stress into passion and energy.

In general, we can use relaxation techniques, exercise, or talk with our friends to help reduce stress on a regular basis.

There will always be some form of stress in your life. It is actually a good thing because it is a signal to prepare or motivate you. You can manage your stress and use it to make you better.

Keep the following in mind to help overcome your stress and anxiety:

Stress is a chemical response designed to motivate and prepare you for life's challenges. You can let the stress ruin you, or you can use it as an initiative to do better.

The first step in reducing your stress is to recognize the thoughts that trigger a stressful reaction in you. Then, identify ways that you can control the thought that makes you feel stressed.

In general, relaxation techniques like breathing exercises, meditation, and counting can help reduce stress. Additionally, helping others, exercising, and performing random acts of kindness can make you feel better about yourself while also reducing your stress.

Pick your favorite concept from this section and share with a friend!

Activity:
Make it your goal to help someone else today. Be on the lookout for the opportunity to hold a door open, buy a coffee, or help a friend at work.

Chapter 5: Nurturing Friendships

"Friendship improves happiness and abates misery, by the doubling of our joy and the dividing of our grief." – Cicero

What You Will Learn in This Chapter:

1. What the 100/0 principle is and why it is crucial to every relationship.
2. Why authenticity helps build strong and trusting relationships.
3. How being present while with friends will allow you to nurture fulfilling friendships.

Introduction to Nurturing Friendships

"Like food and air, we seem to need social relationships to thrive." – Ed Diener, Robert Biswas-Diener

People with close friends are happier. Relationships make us happiest when we feel closely connected. Having friends is important. But having a few close friends we can comfortably share our secrets, small successes or failures with is a key to being happier. It is not the quantity of friends, but the quality. Having people with whom we can discuss our daily thoughts is what makes the difference. Having the most friends on Facebook is not necessarily a good happiness goal, whereas having a few friends with whom we can share ourselves and be authentic with is much more impactful.

We all need our time alone, a break from the world. But the research shows we are happiest when we are with other people. In fact, research on introverts and extroverts found that even introverts who have a natural tendency to be around people less often are still happier when they are with someone they like.

Your happiness also affects other people. You not only can influence your friend's happiness, but you also can influence the happiness of your friend's friends. Happiness works like the spokes on a wheel and radiates outwards throughout your friend connections. It also works in reverse. Surrounding yourself with happy friends positively impacts your happiness. So nurturing friendships is not just good for you; it's good for those around you, and even for those around them.

People with positive friendships tend to be healthier and live longer. They are better suited to deal with stress and rejection. Friends help you get through tough times and even make you smarter. On the contrary, negative relationships detract from both physical and psychological well-being. So, it is worth investing your time and energy in seeking out and maintaining warm, supportive friendships.

Positive friendships require little effort to maintain, and they are definitely worth the investment.

"Friendship redoubleth joys, and cutteth griefs in half." – Francis Bacon

Friendships are an important part of our life. They reduce our stress and help us feel happier. They help us get through tough times, help us be healthier, and even make us smarter. In this section we will share:

1. The secret to every relationship

2. Why it is important to be your authentic self

3. How showing gratitude can improve your friendships

4. How sharing your smiles and hugs help you make and keep friends

5. And finally, we will discuss the importance of just paying attention to your friends.

6. Now let's get started by talking about the importance of your friendships.

Activity:
Schedule time this week to hang out with your friends.

Joyage #19: The Secret to Every Relationship

"Some of the biggest challenges in relationships come from the fact that most people enter a relationship in order to get something: they're trying to find someone who's going to make them feel good. In reality, the only way a relationship will last is if you see your relationship as a place that you go to give, and not a place you go to take." – Anthony Robbins

Positive relationships is one of the strongest concepts supported by the science of happiness. The more and better your relationships are, the happier, healthier, and less stressed you are. A foundational element to creating and improving positive relationships is a concept Al Ritter writes about called the 100/0 principle. Most of us go into a relationship believing that it should be a 50/50 exchange. Two people giving half each, adds up to 100% and then we will all be happy. The challenge is 50/50 doesn't work a lot of the time. If one person gives 50% but the other person only gives 30% because of some challenge they are experiencing in their lives, the relationship suffers.

Give 100% and expect nothing in return. The other person can give 0% and you will still be there for them because you want to give and you believe that your relationship is important. If you have no expectations that they will call you, or bring you flowers, or remember your birthday, or behave in any particular way, you will not have a reason to be disappointed in them and they won't feel pressure to be someone different than they are. Most likely, and even though you are ok if they don't, they will respond in kind. They will appreciate your efforts and they will give more than 0%, and often more than 50% back to the relationship. You will find abundance rather than scarcity in your relationship.

If we give 100% and expect nothing in return, how many of our relationships would be successful? All of them.

Give 100% to the relationship and expect nothing in return. You will find all your relationships flourish and you will feel happier and much less stressed.

Activity:

Pick one relationship to focus on. In this relationship, practice giving 100% without expecting anything in return. Which relationship did you pick? What expectations do you need to let go of in this relationship? What action steps will you take to give all you can?

Joyage #20: Be Authentic

"Be real. Try to do what you say, say what you mean, be what you seem."
– Marian Wright Edelman

In order to develop and maintain friendships, it is important to be authentic. Relationships are closer when people share their personal feelings and challenges. It is about opening up and sharing who you are, the good and the bad, as opposed to simply talking about the weather. It is funny how we are most guarded with the people we are most eager to meet. Going out on a date or meeting with someone we have a tremendous amount of respect for causes us to be on our best behavior and do everything we can to hide our flaws. We go to what sometimes seem like ridiculous lengths to make sure the other person doesn't meet the real us. Usually, that is because we think if they do see the real us, they won't like us.

Brene Brown says we are the "most in debt, addicted, obese, overmedicated adult cohort in us history." We think we can selectively numb ourselves. But when we numb the pain, we also numb the joy. Yet, when asked about our closest relationships, we often explain they are people we can be ourselves with. They are people who accept us for who we are. They are people with whom we can experience our full range of emotions. It is a good idea to make a great first impression. But we should be careful not to overdo the act and pretend to be someone we are not. It can be fun, mysterious, and probably even wise to reveal our secrets and more in-depth thoughts and feelings a little at a time. It is usually a good strategy to show our best qualities first and let them learn about our lesser qualities later. But it is important not to step over the line and pretend to be something we are not. We should be authentic and proud of who we really are, and let that new person decide if they like the real us; if they don't, it is their loss and not ours. Dare to be vulnerable. Be authentic.

Many of us struggle to be vulnerable and to be authentic, because we often believe that our authentic selves may not be good enough.

The first step in creating an environment in which we can be our authentic selves is to build and to invest in friendships that are built on strong foundation of trust. If a relationship lacks trust, it will be difficult to show up authentically.

Activity:
Think of a relationship where you have a lot of trust in the other person. Share something vulnerable with them and see how your friendship grows.

Joyage #21: Just Keep Smiling

"I just like to smile. Smiling's my favorite" – Buddy the Elf

One way to improve your close friendships as well as those in your extended network is to smile more. Smiling is the original example of something going viral. When you smile, other people catch it and they spread it to more people.

Smiling is a built-in mechanism to help us determine if a person is safe. It also gives us the opportunity to quickly determine their emotions. Researchers who suppressed a subject's ability to smile found that they also reduced their ability to read the emotions of others. We automatically mimic someone's smile to determine its authenticity. Smiling is like our internal radar: We send out a smile, and they send a smile back. We mimic that smile and automatically interpret the results. The results enable us to intuitively know whether this person is friend or foe and what kind of mood they are in.

One research study showed that by measuring the smiles of people in their yearbook photos, scientists could predict how long-lasting and fulfilling their lives would be, how they would score on measures of well-being, and how inspiring they would be to others. Other researchers found that measuring smile intensity on a Facebook profile could predict the life satisfaction of college students three-and-a-half years later.

Smiling sends positive messages to the emotional centers in the brain. So even by forcing our faces to smile, we can activate the areas of our brain that make us feel better. In other words, we don't just smile as a result of being happy; smiling actually makes us happier. Smiling also increases mood-enhancing hormones like endorphins and decreases stress-inducing hormones like cortisol, so you become healthier as well as happier. Smiling makes you more attractive to other people and has been correlated with a longer life.

Babies are born smiling. Children smile more than adults. As we get older, we start finding reasons not to smile. We are often so busy trying to be successful or so caught up in being disappointed by the world's lack of perfection and cooperation with our pursuit of success, that we believe we have a lot of reasons not to smile. Stop for a moment and consider this: what would you say if a child asked you why you don't smile a lot? Although your answer may be serious and real, is it really a good reason not to smile?

Smiling improves your happiness and that of your friends. It makes you more approachable and lets people know how you feel about them. One goal might be to try to smile with your eyes. A genuine smile involves the muscles around your mouth, cheeks and eyes. Smile more, with more of your face than just your lips, and you will make new friends and help old friends feel happier and more comfortable around you.

Activity:
Set a reminder on your phone to smile at people today!

Joyage #22: When You're with A Friend... Pay Attention

"The number one predictor of happiness is the time we spend with people we care about and who care about us. The most important source of happiness may be the person sitting next to you. Appreciate them; savor the time you spend together." – Tal Ben-Shahar

When you are with someone, be mindful of them and what they are communicating. What are they trying to get across? Do they want you to learn something? Do they just need to get something off their chest? Are they leaning in with intensity or are they leaning back and very relaxed? Look deep into their eyes. What are their eyes telling you? Take time to be thoughtful and think through what they are saying. Focus on their message by being mindful and observing the whole person. Be fully engaged with them rather than letting your mind wander to everything else in your life or environment. One way to practice being fully engaged in your conversations is to practice active listening. Eliminate any extraneous distractions and listen to the person with an intent to understand. In your efforts to ensure that you are listening fully, make it a practice to reflect back your understanding of what was said. In addition, consider taking your engagement in the conversation to the next level by asking a thoughtful open-ended question of the other person that begins with a "How?, Who?, What?, Where?, or Which?"

Don't check your phone, and definitely don't text someone else during the middle of a conversation. Don't spend your time with them thinking about something else or someone else. Sincerely listen and be involved in their conversation. You will find more enjoyment in the time you spend with them, and they will appreciate your commitment and friendship.

If you pay attention to the people you interact with, they will seek you out and want to talk to you. People want to talk to and spend time with someone they believe will listen and pay attention to them and what they are saying.

Activity:
Next time you are with a friend, commit to being in the moment and thinking only about them. Put your phone away and focus only on them and your conversation.

Closing Thoughts on Nurturing Friendships

"The strongest predictor of happiness is not money, or external recognition through success or fame; it's having meaningful social relationships." – June Gruber, Yale University

Friendships are important for our happiness and they take a little effort to maintain and nurture. Remember the secret to every relationship; give 100% and expect nothing in return. Also, be your authentic self. Spend time with friends who appreciate who you truly are, not who you pretend to be. Be grateful for your friends and show them how grateful you are. We forget sometimes that everyone needs a reminder that they matter and make a difference in our lives. Smiles and hugs are an important part of any relationship. They help start friendships and they remind your friends how important they are without saying a word. Most importantly, pay attention to your friends. When they are talking, act like nothing else in the world is more important than them. Nurture your friendships and they will grow and expand throughout your life.

Right now, reach out to a friend. Make an effort to spend time with your friends and show them how important they are in your world.

Pick your favorite concept from this section and share with a friend!

Chapter 6: Fostering Romantic Relationships

"Love is that condition in which the happiness of another person is essential to your own." — Robert A. Heinlein

What You Will Learn in This Chapter:

1. Why finding the right person isn't enough.
2. Negative habits that may be hurting your relationship.
3. Positive habits that will help make your relationship better.

Introduction to Fostering Romantic Relationships

"The only thing that really matters in life are your relationships to other people... It was the capacity for intimate relationships that predicted flourishing in all aspects of these men's lives." – George Vaillant

Our romantic relationships are often our most impactful to our happiness. Being in a committed relationship means you have to learn to get along with someone else. It gives you someone to share your fears, failures, and successes with. Committed relationships are daily, rather than weekly, and provide a lot of opportunities for small happiness experiences. Romantic relationships create an environment conducive to sharing, intimacy, and the bond of connectedness and that supports being happier.

It matters who you choose to be in a relationship with and what you are focused on getting out of that relationship. So choose carefully and focus on what you can give. Those who find joy in giving to and appreciating their romantic partner are happier than those who focus on what they need and are not getting. As with other aspects of happiness it is the giving which provides the real joy rather than the getting. Relationships are about giving. Once you are focused on giving and not receiving, it becomes much easier to cultivate great relationships.

So, let's get started by learning more about why finding the right person is not enough to have a great relationship.

Joyage #23: Why Finding Your Soulmate Is Not Enough

"A good marriage isn't something you find; it's something you make, and you have to keep on making it." – Gary Thomas

Many people are focused on finding their soulmate with the expectation that once this occurs, they can just be themselves and live happily ever after. Unfortunately, relationships are more complicated than that. Finding your soulmate is a very important beginning, but it is only a beginning. It must be followed up with a commitment to doing a lot of little things on a regular basis to maintain and improve the relationship. Finding opportunities to feel and show appreciation and gratitude, sharing successes and failures, having a sense of humor, working as a team, bringing positive energy to conversations, and regularly saying the small things like "I love you" and "I respect you" all help maintain those positive relationships over time. Positive relationships require effort and commitment. Much of that comes naturally because of our love for the other person; but at some point, as the bloom on the rose fades, a conscious effort is required to build and sustain what can become one of your most important sources of happiness.

In the next few pages we will discuss many ways to build and sustain your most important relationships.

Activity:
Think about your best friend. Now think about the work and effort it takes on both parts to maintain your friendship.

Joyage #24: Relationships and The Positivity Ratio

"Successful people build each other up. They motivate, inspire, and push each other. Unsuccessful people just hate, blame, and complain." –
Unknown

We often take for granted that our partners or friends know we love them. We have said it hundreds of times and we show it through the many things we do with and for them. But they still need to hear it said aloud often. Relationships require constant confirmation that things are going well. We tend to get into a habit of assuming the good and talking about the bad. Have you ever said this to yourself or someone else: "Of course, he knows I love him. That is why I married him. We need to talk about why he doesn't open up to me." We think about and appreciate the unique and wonderful traits about the other person, but we don't always give voice to those thoughts. So even though we are thinking of them and they are a part of our internal conversation, our significant other doesn't get to hear them. They only hear the part we have time (or decide to make time) to talk about, which can often be the problems or challenges rather than the things we are grateful for.

Research on several different levels has shown that relationships need more positive input than negative input. This is called your "Positivity Ratio." John Gottman found that personal relationships need at least five positive comments, actions, or statements for every one negative comment. The real challenge is that our habits are usually to voice the negative and assume the positive. We love and appreciate the other person, and we assume they know it. It is not bothering us, so we don't feel the need to make sure we express those positive feelings. On the other hand, we feel like we need to express the negative feelings. We need to get them out, hash them out, or somehow expel them from our mind. So, once we get comfortable in a relationship, we tend to speak the negative and assume the positive.

By consciously focusing on the positivity ratio, we realize that we have to work hard to get to five to one. The good news is that even though it is difficult, we can build the habits of positivity that will make our relationships stronger.

Activity:
Give more positive feedback than negative feedback. For one day, use an index card or your Notes App on your smartphone and add a little tick mark every time you say something positive about the other person in your relationship. Count how often you tell them you appreciate them.

Joyage #25: Negative Habits That Are Hurting Your Relationship

"Any fool can criticize, condemn, and complain – and most fools do. But it takes character and self-control to be understanding and forgiving." – Dale Carnegie

Most people are not aware of the habits and patterns they have formed in their relationships.

One of the best-known researchers on marriage and romantic relationships, John Gottman, has honed the ability to determine the health of a relationship within the first five minutes of observing a couple interact. His methods have resulted in an ability to predict which couples will last with 90% accuracy.

Here are the negative habits Gottman recommends we avoid to make our relationships better.

Fight these negative habits:
1. Criticizing - Don't criticize or point out flaws in your partner's character or personality.
2. Defensiveness - Listen and consider the meaning of what your spouse is saying rather than potentially hurtful words he or she is using. Avoid denying responsibility, blaming someone or something else, whining, or being the victim. Negative statements that begin with "You always..." and "You never..." are indicators of challenges if the accompanying tone of voice is also negative.
3. Don't use contempt or disgust – Don't talk down to your spouse as if you are superior. Don't insult, use sarcasm, mock the other person, show disapproval, judgment, or hostile humor, or communicate that the other person is incompetent. The amount of disgust shown on a partner's face can be used

to predict the health of the relationship and the amount of time a couple will be separated.

4. Stonewalling – withdrawing emotionally. Don't exit the room or the conversation. Don't start watching TV, looking at your phone, or reading a book during the middle of a serious conversation.

5. Whining – statements that blame the other person and make you the victim as if you did not have any control. Don't complain when you can make a request.

For many of us, these are bad habits that we are not even aware of.

Activity:
Spend a day observing your interactions with your soulmate and see if any of these show up. You can also have an honest talk with them and ask if they are noticing any of these habits. Don't try to become perfect and fix everything. For one month, pick one negative habit to focus on. When you notice a negative interaction, think about the trigger and how to avoid it. Then apologize and keep trying.

Joyage #26: Positive Habits That Will Improve Your Relationship

"Try to use the pronoun 'we' instead of 'you,' and speak about the intended result instead of the failed attempt." – Terri Lonier

Most people are not aware of the habits and patterns they have formed in their relationships.

We talked about John Gottman and the negative habits he lists that we should avoid in the prior Joyage. Here are the positive habits Gottman recommends we implement to make our relationships better.

Create these good habits to nurture positive relationships:

1. Use "we" instead of "I" to show you are in this together and to help reduce the perception of blame.

2. Have a sense of humor – be able to laugh at yourself. Insert humor into tense situations to hint to your partner that, no matter what, you still care about him or her.

3. Start every conversation with something positive rather than jumping into negative statements.

4. Listen to and support each other's hopes and dreams. Our hopes and dreams give us a true sense of purpose; and at the same time, they are areas of great sensitivity and low confidence. Knowing our hopes and dreams are honored and respected gives us renewed strength and makes the relationship extraordinarily valuable. Not supporting the other person's hopes and dreams can lead to a slow death of the relationship as the other person slowly builds the

confidence to pursue his or her dreams and leave the non-supporting partner behind.

5. Start discussions by clarifying what you do agree with before jumping into what you don't agree with.

6. Say small positive things often: Thank you, I love you, I respect you, I like you.

You probably already do a lot of these naturally. It is what has helped maintain your relationship so far.

Activity:
Find one habit from the list you want to improve. Practice it with your partner, every day for 30 days.

Joyage #27: Work on The Small Moments

"The best portion of your life will be the small, nameless moments you spend smiling with someone who matters to you." – Unknown

John Gottman, considered one of the foremost researchers on relationships, tells a story about a time when he was walking by his wife and he saw her looking into the mirror sadly. He knew he had two choices: he could keep going and go read a book that he was very interested in, or he could stop and listen to a story he wasn't sure he wanted to hear. Which would you have chosen?

Understanding that relationships are based on the trust that is built during these tiny moments, he stopped, listened, and connected with his wife.

To nurture positive relationships, we can take advantage of those small moments and fleeting opportunities. These help us build trust with others. Brene Brown, in her book <u>Daring Greatly</u>, used the analogy of marbles in a marble jar. Each time we take a moment to connect, we are putting marbles in a marble jar. The marbles represent the good will we may need later when our actions are less than positive and we need forgiveness and understanding from our partner or friends. It is like our positive relationship savings account. We are saving for later, when the relationship will need the trust or forgiveness that we have built up over time.

Activity:

Pick one of the following activities try it for the next 30 days:

1. Create rituals that give you the opportunity to connect
   - Dinner with the family
   - Annual vacations
   - Nightly walks
   - Activities related to common interests: exercise, diet, gardening, bowling, saving money for a big purchase

2. Talk a lot
   - Talk about things you appreciate about the other person
   - Talk about small things the person is going to be doing each day
   - Share and discuss the positive aspects of experiences
   - Talk about and be excited for the small wins in each of your lives.

Joyage #28: Perfection & Apologies

"Don't worry about getting perfect, just keep getting better." – Frank Peretti

We are human beings, so we are not perfect. We can't always give 100% and make all our important relationships work. As a matter of fact, it is difficult to get it right more than 50% of the time. Relationships are emotionally charged and full of surprises and difficult moments. But that doesn't mean we give up. We try to be the best person we can be today, and then we build from there. When we make mistakes, we forgive ourselves, apologize to the other person, and work on doing better. It might be hard to apologize, because often the other person had some involvement in what went wrong, and we don't want to move forward without them recognizing their role. But that is counterproductive and doesn't fit with the 100/0 Principle. We are giving 100%, so we need to own it and apologize for our actions, no matter what the other person does. Over the years we will improve and get better, but we will always have times when we are imperfect and we need to forgive ourselves, apologize, and try to do better. Knowing we will be wrong and will fail will also help us accept those missteps in everyone else. Because we've forgiven ourselves, we can forgive them, help them forgive themselves, support them, and move forward.

Activity:
Pick one mistake you have made in your relationship and forgive yourself for it. Acknowledge your mistake and move forward. Now reach out to the other person who was affected and apologize. Let them know you made a mistake and you want to do better. Don't have any expectations about their response. Just give the apology sincerely and move forward.

Joyage #29: Don't Ever Tolerate Abuse in A Relationship

"When someone isn't treating you right, no matter how much you love them, you've got to love yourself more and walk away." – Unknown

There is a line between not having expectations and allowing someone to abuse us. Giving us flowers, fixing us dinner, remembering our birthdays, or turning off the TV to talk to us are some expectations of things that people do when they care for us. We can eliminate these expectations and improve our relationships, however we shouldn't eliminate the expectation that other people will treat us with the respect and dignity that we deserve. The key differentiation is the distinction between what people do "for us," which is good and which we should allow them to control, and what people do "to us" in a negative form, which is against us and could hurt us.

Our tolerance level for verbal, physical, or any other kind of abuse should be something close to zero. For example, we may not like that someone around us uses curse words in their language, but that is their choice. We should not start setting expectations that they can or can't curse. We could choose to be around it or not, and we can communicate to them how we feel about cursing, but they get to choose whether or not they want to curse. If someone is cursing at us in an abusive way, our tolerance level changes. They are doing something negative "to us" and causing us harm, and we need to immediately remove ourselves from that situation. If the answer is yes to any of these questions, you should remove yourself and find a safer situation.

Click Help on the Joyages app for additional helpful resources:

- Do you ever fear for yours or someone else's safety?
- Do you consistently feel humiliated or embarrassed?
- Is your partner rude, or hypercritical to the point of being rude?

Activity:

Ask yourself the questions above about a relationship you're in. Evaluate your relationship and if the answer to any of the questions is "yes," remove yourself from the relationship immediately.

Joyage #30: Get Excited About Good News

"To multiply your happiness, share it with others" – Unknown

Respond well to good news. It can make your relationship stronger and help it last longer. Research has shown that our happiness is magnified when we can share it with others, and magnified even further if the other person has a positive and enthusiastic response to our happiness. How your partner responds to good news is a better predictor of the longevity of the relationship than how he or she responds to bad news. Celebrating small wins is ideally something you encounter daily, or at least much more often than you encounter hard times. Sharing small wins with the people who are close to us increases our level of happiness associated with those wins. Just as importantly, when others share wins with us it is important to respond positively and enthusiastically. We can often dampen their level of happiness by responding negatively or even by responding in a neutral manner.

Good news is an opportunity for someone close to you to share their excitement about big or small accomplishments. People who are good with children do this naturally: When a child walks up and proudly shows them how they tied their own shoe or finished a puzzle with six pieces, they get noticeably excited and share their feeling of accomplishment with the child. It is a celebration for something that may seem small to an adult observer, but it is significant to the child. They work to find more accomplishments they can show off. When we become adults, we don't lose that need or that desire to share our great news and little wins with other people. So how we handle those opportunities in a relationship is important, especially when someone shares with us. Dismissing them as menial or something that should have already been accomplished takes away that joy. So does talking over their news and telling them about our lives, because we just can't wait to get it out. Taking time to appreciate, compliment, and celebrate their little successes and news is just as important for adults as it is for children. Those close connections are formed in the small interactions around good news and small accomplishments. These small acts show that we value them, and that what happens in their lives is important to us.

Activity:

Remember some of the things your significant other has told you about and ask them about the outcomes. Check in to find out how things went. If they took the time to tell you about it, then it is of special meaning or importance to them. Follow up in a positive and participatory manner to show them they matter to you.

Closing Thoughts on How to Improve Your Relationships

Remember, relationships are important for reducing stress and building a strong foundation for being happier. It is not just the people involved - everyone has to work at creating and maintaining positive relationships. The secret to every relationship is the 100/0 principle. Always give 100% and don't expect anything in return. All of your relationships will work if you follow this important principle. Successful relationships require you to recognize and reduce your negative habits and increase your positive habits. 5 positives for every negative is a great rule of thumb. Finally, remember to get excited about your partner's good news and pause to connect in those small moments. The small moments add up and become a foundation for a stronger relationship.

Relationships are about giving. Once you are focused on giving and not receiving, it becomes much easier to cultivate great relationships.

So, let's build a habit of giving that improves our closest relationship. Make a commitment to implement the 100/0 Principle over the next 30 days. Find ways to give and expect nothing in return.

Keep the following in mind to help you foster romantic relationships:

Finding your soulmate is important, but maintaining a healthy relationship goes way beyond finding the right person. Commit to maintaining and improving the relationship daily by expressing gratitude, sharing successes and failures, having a sense of humor, working as a team, bringing positive energy to conversations, and regularly saying the small things like "I love you" and "I respect you."

Fight the negative habits of your relationship such as criticizing your partner, being defensive, using contempt or disgust, stonewalling or whining. By refusing to act on these behaviors, your relationship will become more positive.

Create positive habits that will help your relationship improve. Use "we" instead of "I", begin conversations positively, have a sense of humor, and support your partner's dreams. Take one of these habits and practice it daily for the next thirty days.

Pick your favorite concept from this section and share with a friend!

Chapter 7: Managing Work and Career

"It is neither wealth nor splendor, but tranquility and occupation, which give happiness." – Thomas Jefferson

What You Will Learn in This Chapter:

1. How to find purpose in your work.
2. The difference between a job and a career, and how to find happiness regardless.
3. How to manage and improve all your work relationships.

Introduction to Work and career

"There are many days I don't feel like training, but there is never a day when I feel like losing." – Serena Williams

What is your favorite part of your job? Is it the paycheck? Or is it the satisfaction of knowing you are contributing to something great? Studies on happiness show that people who find meaning and purpose in their work feel less stressed and more fulfilled in their lives than people who just "punch in and punch out."

If you think about it, this makes sense, doesn't it? A full-time job takes up almost half our waking hours. If finding meaning at work means you can spend half of your life as happily as you do at home, well, that's definitely worth investing in!

Your purpose at your job can be greater than the tasks you perform if you let it. If you aren't feeling a connection right now between meaning and your work, there's a lot you can do to shift your mindset. The key is to think about how your unique strengths and values have an impact on the service you provide.

You can do this even if the job you are in right now is not your ideal job. You can always bring a higher purpose to what you are doing right now, no matter what it is. For example, if your goal is to be an entrepreneur someday but you are flipping burgers today, you can be proud that you are learning a lot about customer service and about what it feels like to put a smile on someone's face each day. You can experience how meaningful it feels to be valued as part of a team. Every career step you make is taking you a step closer to being a more fulfilled you.

1. Try some Find a connection between your company's goals and values and your own. Does your company provide a much-needed service or a make a product that makes people happy? Think of the big picture as you contribute to that each day.

2. Think positively about your accomplishments. Take a minute at the end of each work day to write down all that you completed and the impact that had on your team and your customers.

3. Volunteer. Many companies do valuable work in the community and you can join them in that mission.

4. Help someone else. Whether it is collaborating with a teammate or teaching a trainee, it feels good to help others succeed by sharing your skills.

You have nothing to lose by giving these mindset shifts a try. Your job can be much bigger than yourself if you bring purpose to it!

Activity:
Write down 5 of your top strengths. For each strength you have, write down how it can make an impact on the service you provide.

Joyage #31: Job Vs. Career

"Your career is what you're paid for. Your calling is what you're made for."
– Steve Harvey

How do you feel about your job? Is it a chore? Or is it something more rewarding? Studies show that a big part of life satisfaction is job satisfaction. People who look at their work as "just a job," simply aren't as happy as people who see their job as a "calling."

Your mindset about your job isn't necessarily about the work you do, but your attitude toward it. In other words, it's not about what you do, but about how you do it. Want to take your temperature on how you feel about your job? Think about these scenarios and see what resonates with you.

What motivates and excites you about your job? Is it just your paycheck and meeting all your commitments every month? Does your day go too slowly? Do you live for the weekends? If so, you are probably stuck in a job mindset. You need a job to pay your bills and you clock in, do your best, and clock out.

On the other hand, are you motivated by promotions and bonuses at work? Do you see your job as a steppingstone to a future goal you have? Do you invest a lot of extra hours to get ahead? If so, you are probably in a career mindset. Having a career mindset isn't a bad thing at all. It's good to have goals and to want to hone your skills. But staying in this mindset too long will mean you fall short of bringing a higher purpose to what you do.

Finally, do you love what you do? Does work not feel like work at all, but a rewarding part of your daily life? Does time fly when you are working? Does your work leave you satisfied about your contribution to others and to your team? If so, congratulations, because you have a calling. A calling brings meaning and purpose to everything you do.

When you have a calling, you have a higher motivation than your paycheck. You are thinking about the impact you will have on the world.

Being in a calling mindset gives you a special kind of satisfaction. It just makes you happier to get up in the morning. Now, if you aren't there yet, don't worry. Try this exercise to see if it can bring you a step closer:

Sit down and rewrite your job description as if you are enticing someone else to do it. Talk about how your job impacts others and how your interactions with your coworkers fulfills your mission in life. If you are an employer or manager, rewrite the job descriptions of your employees or team too. See what you can do to make them feel like you all have a collective purpose to latch on to. In doing that, not only will you make your employees happier, but you may just find it helps you see your own calling too.

If you put your mind to it, you can change the way you think about the tasks that you like and what you don't like. You can begin to see yourself in the bigger picture, doing some good in the world. When you bring meaning and purpose to your job, you will always have more energy to tackle the day ahead.

Activity:
Sit down and rewrite your job description as if you are enticing someone else to do it. Talk about how your job impacts others and how your interactions with your coworkers fulfills your mission in life. If you are an employer or manager, rewrite the job descriptions of your employees or team too.

Joyage #32: When Times Are Tough at Work, Make Your Relationships Your Priority

"Like food and air, we seem to need social relationships to thrive" – Diener

Unfortunately for many of us, our natural inclination when things start to go wrong is to abandon our relationships and go it alone. We do this for many reasons. Stress clouds our thought. We focus on the goal of fixing the problem and don't have time to reach out for other opinions. We don't want to admit our challenges or failures. The problem is, during a crisis is when we need other people the most. It is when we need a clear, objective point of view to help us make decisions, and we need their emotional support because the stress and worry exhausts our emotional resources. Busyness and stress cause us to shut out the people we love just when we need them the most.

One of the fallacies most of us embrace is that there will only be one crisis, one failure, or one tough project we have to power through. So we think that if we focus all our attention on the situation and temporarily give up the things that matter to us, like time with our friends and family, we will get past this hill and be able to get back to our normal routines. But that small hill is part of a mountain range, and one hill will lead to a bigger hill. Our reward for climbing the hill so successfully is a bigger hill, then an even bigger hill, and eventually a mountain. There will always be tough times; they are an important part of our lives. But if we make our relationships a priority, we will always have the support we need to keep pushing and keep enjoying the good times in life that will also always be there for us.

I once saw a story about a mountain climber who was in a dire situation. He had lost his partner to a fall and now had to get out of a crevice by himself before dark, or risk being buried by falling snow or possibly freezing to death. He had made it to a ledge and only had about 20 more feet to climb. He had often completed similar climbs using only his hands, without any ropes or support, on the climbing walls in the gym. Climbing free hand should only take 5 to 10 minutes. If he took his time and invested in fastening all of the supports and safety techniques as he had been taught, it could take as long as an hour to make the same climb. The risk was, without the support system, if he slipped, he would fall 500 feet to his death in the chasm and no one would know.

Which have you chosen? Do you have the patience to build the support system or are you risking everything to get there as fast as possible? What if you knew there would be another challenge at the end of that climb? Your positive relationships are your support system. If you ignore them, your happiness and level of success are constantly at risk. If you take the time to build those positive relationships, you will have many opportunities to successfully reach the peak of happiness and success.

The climber chose to build the support system, mostly because the past warnings of his fallen partner still rang in his ear. He made it to the top, only to lose his grip just as he was climbing over the edge. Luckily, the support system he had taken the time to create did its job and kept him from falling more than a few feet. He was able to regain his grip, climb over the edge, and live to tell his story.

Invest in your relationships. The support structure will serve you well when the stress of work and life seems overwhelming.

Activity:
Engage with your coworkers outside of the office. Invite them to lunch, dinner, or even a quick walk during the day. Build relationships that you can trust when times get tough.

Joyage #33: Why Are Work Relationships Important?

"...work relationships are central, not only for how work gets done, but also for the quality of our lives." – Dutton and Ragins

Not only are relationships important for happiness in our personal lives, they are also important for happiness at work. For most people, happiness at work is complemented by dynamic interpersonal relationships, which include ongoing respect and recognition for accomplishing something meaningful. Given that most of us spend 50% or more of our waking hours at work, it would be impossible to ignore the impact of relationships in that area of our lives. In the past, relationships at work have been a taboo subject because of how complicated they are and how complicated they can make productivity and work life in general when they go from good to bad, which seems to happen often.

Unfortunately, relationships are a vital part of our work lives and productivity, and ignoring their existence is no longer productive. Our best solution is to understand the nature of work relationships and teach employees and team members how to create and sustain positive relationships. Most everything we do at work runs more smoothly when we have positive relationships and the related support at work. In the workplace, happy people receive more support than less happy people.

Happy people get more done because they have team members who can add knowledge or lend a hand. We are happier because we have people to commiserate with and to discuss and test our feelings with. Our relationships with vendors and clients determine our ability to bring new ideas and get raises and promotions. In the modern work environment, having other people to help us focus and expand our knowledge allows us to be more productive and more creative.

Activity:
Write down a list of your important relationships at work and how you can cultivate them.

Joyage #34: A Good Relationship with Your Boss Is Important

"You will never be a leader unless you first learn to follow and be led." –
Tiorio

Our relationship with our supervisor is the number one predictor of our willingness to stay at our job and has a significant impact on our happiness and success.

Who does your review, decides on your raises, and hands out all the best projects? Who has the most influence on your day to day happiness and success at your job?

The next steps in your career, to a large extent, will be determined by your boss and more accurately, by your relationship with your boss. Your boss is not perfect, but neither are you. Forget their imperfections, no matter how blatant and annoying they may be. Your career depends on it.

Create a personal relationship with your boss. Schedule lunch with them. Ask them about their families, careers, and hobbies. What is important to them? What do you have in common? The more ways you can connect, the better you will understand them and the easier it will become to work with them. Ask about their expectations and do your best to deliver on them. Be a great employee so it will be easy for them to be a great boss.

Recognize that they are people too. They have strengths and weaknesses, fears and insecurities, and hopes and dreams. Help them be happy and successful. Find time to be their friend.

Find ways to have a positive relationship with your supervisor and you will be happier and more successful.

Activity:
Schedule time to get lunch or grab coffee with your boss. Try not to talk about work, but about what they like to do outside the office. Get to know them!

Joyage #35: Dealing with Bad Bosses

"People don't leave bad jobs, they leave bad bosses." – Unknown

We all have bad bosses at some point in our career. For many of us, it may be for as much as 50% or more of our working lives. Successful people find ways to deal with, learn from, and become friends with their supervisors, even the bad ones. What can you do to be happy and successful even if you have a bad boss?

1. Recognize they are human. Believe it or not, they were not put on this earth just to make our lives miserable. Bosses are people and they have faults just like we do. They also have fears and insecurities, as well as hopes and dreams. What are they scared of or worried about that is driving their behaviors? How can you be more understanding and helpful with their challenges?

2. Get to know them as a person, not just a boss. Go to lunch or schedule time on your calendars to get to know each other; ask about their families, careers, hobbies, and lives in general. What is important to them? What do you have in common? The more ways you can connect, the better you will understand them and the easier it will become to work with them.

3. Don't be the victim. Don't let one person, even if they are your supervisor, ruin your day. No matter what they do, you get to choose how you react to them.

4. Put yourself in their shoes. Why are they asking you to do certain things? What types of stresses and challenges are they under? What kind of pressure are they getting from their boss? What would you expect from your position if you were the

boss? Deliver for them at the same level you would expect an employee to deliver for you.

5. You can't change them. Accept them for who they are, with all their flaws and challenges. Focus on appreciating what is good about them rather than trying to change what you judge as bad.

6. Recognize your autonomy. You can always quit your job or find some other role within the company. In most situations, you are better off learning how to adapt to a bad boss rather than running away from the situation.

How we choose to relate to our bosses can have a significant impact on our happiness and success. We can spend our time ruminating about our "bad boss" and letting them wreak havoc on our emotions, or we can choose to be happy and successful no matter what the situation. Take control of your life. Find ways to have a positive relationship with your supervisor, no matter what kind of boss they are.

Activity:
Think of a few positive traits or skillsets that you could learn from your boss and write them down. This will help change your mindset when thinking of your boss.

Joyage #36: How to Improve Your Work Relationships

"the strongest predictor of happiness is not money, or external recognition through success or fame; it's having meaningful social relationships." – *June Gruber*

High Quality Connections are short, mutually positive interactions. They can occur in very short periods of time, but they leave people feeling energized and important. People with High Quality Connections show less negative impacts from stressful situations, and they seem to be able to weather the storm more calmly.

People with High Quality Connections also live longer. They are sick less often and have lower blood pressure., partly because high quality connections release oxytocin, which is like a relationship hormone that reduces stress and increases a person's willingness to cooperate. They can help people explore and confirm roles within a group so they have an identity that matters to them and is of value to the team. People with High Quality Connections have more physical zest, energy, and vitality. They have more resilience, and they learn faster, and they are even better at identifying who they are and how they fit in, which helps them be more effective change agents.

High quality connections can be created in short, focused interactions. By recognizing the value of positive relationships and their significant impact on productivity, and making it a priority to create such relationships, we can pause and focus on the person who is requesting our attention. Stop your work, look up from the computer screen, and acknowledge the presence of another human being. Listen intently to what they are trying to communicate and respond actively and positively. A 30-second interaction can have an impact on their psyche that will last all day long. You get to decide if you will make that impact positive and productive or negative and demotivating. A series of positive, people-focused interactions will build good will that will help the team push through future challenges.

So now that we know the value, how can you create High Quality Connections? Start by engaging with people when they come into your workspace. Stop what you are doing and give them your full attention. Don't fall victim to "disrespectful engagement." It makes you less energized, less motivated, and less committed. Use mutual positive regard, trust, and active engagement to help team members feel more open, competent, and energized. Give them your attention, be authentic, listen attentively, and actively respond to the discussion. If you don't have time, let them know when a better time will be.

Be aware of and practice High Quality Connections and you will significantly improve your positive relationships at work.

Activity:
Pick a day and focus all your attention on every interaction with a person. Put down your phone, turn or close your computer screen, and don't look at or answer your phone. Look only at them and pay attention to what they are saying and how they are saying it. A little practice and you will become an expert at High Quality Connections.

Joyage #37: No Room for Blaming in The Workplace

"Blaming others takes time and energy from improving yourself." –
Anonymous

Blaming can quickly interfere with our positive relationships at work as well as sabotage our success and happiness. In every work environment there are things that go wrong and things that go right. There may be challenges with our coworkers, our boss may not behave as we like, or the vendors may not come through on an important project. We can focus on blaming someone, or we can focus on fixing the problem. Often, we blame people simply because they didn't do what we would have expected them to do or what we would have done. More often than not, we never give those explanations to them, nor do we spend enough time to give them the tools to get it done. We may have years of experience packed into our brains; and we expect that everyone else has the same perspective, even though they may have only been at the company a few months. We don't realize how much we know just from experience and how much a newer team member may not have learned yet. Very few people want things to go poorly at work, and so part of creating positive relationships is doing whatever is necessary to help the other person continue to learn. Rather than wasting our time blaming someone, we can accept the situation and take action to improve it now and in the future. This is part of taking control of our lives. When we blame someone, we give them control; we become victims. When we accept and find solutions, we become empowered to create our own happiness and success.

Activity:
Next time an issue arises at work, focus on fixing the problem, rather than finding someone to blame. If you happen to know who caused the problem, explain to them what they could do better, and guide them through resolving the issue.

Joyage #38: A Key to Great Workplace Relationships: Recognize and Appreciate

"Celebrate what you want to see more of." – Tom Peters

A great habit for creating positive relationships at work is providing recognition. Recognize people for great work, for taking the first step, for making a great effort, and for anything else we can find. Sometimes we think that because it is work, we should only point out what people are doing wrong, but that may hurt more than it helps.

Think about coaching a kids soccer team. When kids are five, they don't know anything about soccer; so we don't wait until one of them scores a goal to get excited. We are excited when they just touch the ball. Then we get more excited when they actually kick the ball. We recognize them when they kick the ball in the right direction, and then we recognize them again when they kick the ball in the right direction two or three times in a row. If we only pointed out that they didn't score, they would never learn. Many of the kids don't score any goals their first season. We would never think about not recognizing the small accomplishments they did make. Adults are no different.

Adults try hard to learn new things and will make mistakes early in the process. We can recognize what someone else did well, or we can wait until they get everything perfect. The first method encourages them to continue working hard to get better, and the second method leaves them discouraged and unhappy. Some people have been beaten down so much in their lives that they are uncomfortable with recognition – even positive! They dodge it and sometimes appear to shun it. But it is lighting a small fire inside them that even they might not recognize; and in time, they will come to appreciate and even expect to hear a few positive words from you. Ultimately, they will be loyal and more hard-working because of it. Recognize people for the little things, and recognize them often. It is one of the best ways to create positive relationships.

Activity:

Practice Recognition at Work - Here are 3 actions you can take to practice recognition:

1. Find team members and tell them what a great job they are doing.
2. Send an email to their boss or their team.
3. Recognize your supervisor or his or her boss as well. All levels of team members need recognition.

Joyage #39 Eliminate Expectations

"When you stop expecting people to be perfect, you can like them for who they are."—Donald Miller

One common challenge with supervisor/employee relationships is that we expect our bosses to do or be certain things. For example, we expect them to be leaders, make good decisions, recognize us for our efforts, explain how they want things done, and to clearly communicate their expectations. Unfortunately, our bosses are similar to us and may not have been trained or prepared to meet these expectations. Most supervisors are promoted because they are good at their job rather than because they would make good bosses. So, they don't understand our expectations or know how to deliver on them.

Managing Our Expectations of Our Bosses

1. Write at the top of blank sheet of paper, "I expect my boss to:"
2. Then make a list of your expectations.
3. Put a star next to the most important expectations.
4. Now cross out "I expect my boss to:" and write in "I would be grateful if my boss were to:" Now you have a list of what you will appreciate if it happens rather than what you will be angry about when it doesn't happen.
5. For the expectations you starred, sit down and talk to your boss. Courteously ask them if they can help in those areas. Be ready to discuss how they can help.

You can spend your time appreciating the good things that your boss does or being angry about unmet expectations. The first is productive and helpful; the second is a waste of your time and energy.

Activity:

Schedule lunch or coffee with your boss. Bring your list and have a friendly conversation. Be sure to ask how you can add value to the company and to their success.

Closing Thoughts on Work and Career

Use mindset shifting to find purpose in your work. Find a connection between your company's goals and values and your own, think positively about your accomplishments, volunteer, or help someone else to help you find purpose and motivation at your job.

Think to yourself about your job. Are you there just for the paycheck, or do you feel satisfied and find purpose in your work? This is the difference between a job and a career. Rewrite your job description to make it sound enticing to others. Think about how your purpose at your job aligns with your purpose in life. You'll begin to see the bigger picture and have more energy and excitement about going to work.

Connect and devote your full attention to others, avoid blame in the workplace, and practice recognition to improve and build positive relationships in your workplace.

Work relationships are critical to your happiness and success. Your two most important relationships at work are with your boss and a work "best friend." Reach out to people at work on a personal level. Remember that your boss is a person too, and don't set unreasonable expectations for them that leave you unhappy and stressed. There are bad bosses out there but there are also many techniques for turning bad situations into positive ones. It is important to nurture relationships that will help you deal with the stresses and strains of work. Remember not to waste your time blaming and make sure you create a habit of recognizing and appreciating all of your team members. Finally, engage with your team members when they are present. Find those moments when you can build trust and High-Quality Connections.

So, let's create a positive habit: Schedule one lunch per week for the next month. Three with team members and one with your boss. At each lunch meeting, think of one action they have taken that helps the team and thank them for it. Get to know them personally and help them get to know you.

Pick your favorite concept from this chapter and share with a friend!

Chapter 8: Practicing Mindfulness

"Do not dwell in the past, do not dream of the future, concentrate the mind on the present moment." —Buddha

What You'll Learn in This Chapter:
1. How mindfulness helps you live in the present.
2. Mindfulness isn't meditation or mindlessness.
3. Practicing mindfulness can also help you practice gratitude.

Introduction to Practicing Mindfulness

"Mindfulness is simply being aware of what is happening right now without wishing it were different; enjoying the pleasant without holding on when it changes (which it will); being with the unpleasant without fearing it will always be this way (which it won't)." – James Baraz

Mindfulness has become a buzzword in our culture, and you can hear many people exclaiming its benefits. But what exactly is Mindfulness?

Mindfulness is the ability to remove the distractions of what might happen or what did happen and focus on what is happening right now this second. It also includes being curious and open to discovering new inspirations and information in the current setting.

As a society we tend to place a high regard on our ability to multi-task. The challenge is that research shows that multi-tasking doesn't really work. We tend to shift between multiple tasks quickly and for short periods of time. This causes us to eliminate parts of the task in order to quickly shift in and out of it. The parts we are eliminating include focus, thoughtfulness, and appreciation. Instead of living in "the moment" we are attempting to live in several moments at the same time.

Think of one of the most common and rude forms of multi-tasking: We are having a conversation with a person and we receive, read, and answer a text while they are talking. We are physically in the same space as the person and we probably get the overall idea of what they are saying. But we miss the opportunity to connect with them, to stop and really think about what they are communicating to us.

Most importantly, we are not allowing time to stop and appreciate the here and now of our lives. We are focused on the message on our phone, which is often trivial, in comparison to our feelings about the person with whom we are actually visiting. The result is we go from activity to activity throughout a day or a week and our memories are not of the great moments in our lives, but rather about how busy we have been. We have missed our opportunities for happiness by attempting to do everything, rather than choosing the few things that will make us happy and productive.

Mindfulness has several levels: it can be as simple as being aware of nature during a walk, or very involved like meditation where you are focusing your mind, spirit, and body.

As we go through the activities in our lives, are we worried about the future, fretting and reliving the past, or are we focused on what we can enjoy, learn from and appreciate right now? Do we value the text that is planning our next interaction with someone more than we value the present interaction? Or are we so busy planning and thinking about what we need or want to do to be happy that we are not finding the happiness available right now in front of us. James Oppenheim said "The Foolish man seeks happiness in the distance; the wise man grows it under his feet." Mindfulness is about looking at what is around us and under our feet, rather than worrying about the future.

Activity:
We are sometimes afraid to be alone with our thoughts, waste time, or worse yet, appear to not be productive or engaged. Next time you get this feeling, you can become productive by being mindful and appearing to do nothing: Observe the people around you and the environment. What parts of your surroundings can you appreciate? Look at the details. What can you notice that you have never seen before?

Joyage #40: Five Common Myths About Mindfulness

"Mindfulness is not about getting anywhere else." – Jon Kabat-Zinn

So, we talked a little about what mindfulness can be. Now let's discuss what mindfulness is not.

First, mindfulness is not meditation.

The two terms mindfulness and meditation often get thrown around interchangeably. But mindfulness is an awareness. It's paying attention, on purpose, in the present moment, without judgment. You don't need a meditation cushion, or even more than a split second, to be mindful. Dr. Jon Kabat-Zinn, one of the first American mindfulness researchers, likens mindfulness to being behind a waterfall. You're not under the waterfall, caught in the swirl and pounding of thoughts, emotions, and sensations, nor are you trying to stop or change them. Instead, you're behind the cascade, observing all that's happening without evaluation.

Meditation, by contrast, is a practice. It's all the awareness that is mindfulness, but sustained for a period of time. Rather than just checking in with the waterfall, it's logging some time behind it. It's bringing your attention back when it inevitably wanders away, often many times a minute.

Next, mindfulness is not taking time out to relax.

Mindfulness isn't relaxation. Stress reduction may be a side effect; checking in with your thoughts, body, and impulses decreases your chance of getting pulled around by them, which in turn lightens your stress considerably. But fundamentally, mindfulness isn't rest; indeed, the two are apples and oranges. Even remembering to be mindful can take quite a bit of work. But many people find that checking in with their thoughts, feelings, and sensations, even if it's not necessarily restorative, is definitely illuminating.

Mindfulness is not mindlessness. The idea that mindfulness requires a blank mind is a myth that makes many people believe they can't be mindful. But just like you can't stop your heart from beating or your stomach from digesting, you can't stop your brain from thinking. That's what it does.

Think about it this way: mindfulness isn't a suspension of thoughts; instead, it's a suspension of judgment. Put another way, mindfulness is an observation of what's happening: that itch above your left eyebrow, the bad taste in your mouth, the realization that the thought that you're a bad daughter is nothing more than a thought, or the fact that the Kit Kat jingle has been running through your head for the better part of a minute.

Mindfulness welcomes any and all thoughts, but tries to see them as just that: thoughts. As one popular bumper sticker sums up: Don't believe everything you think.

Mindfulness is not forever. It's impossible to be in the present moment at all times. Sometimes you need to plan for the future: "What's for dinner?" or "I can feel a migraine coming on—I should really take some medicine, drink some coffee, and go lie down." It's also important to reflect on the past: "Next time I'll actually try to listen rather than shooting off my mouth," or "Ugh, I shouldn't have eaten those leftover pork dumplings."

Being aware of everything in the present moment all the time isn't just impossible, it would leave us overstimulated and exhausted. Even mindfulness gurus have many mindless moments—getting lost in rumination or daydreaming.

Finally, mindfulness isn't always bliss. This is a tough one. Mindfulness is not simply savoring the moment, taking time to notice the hues of a sunset, or the taste of that warm chocolate chip cookie, or the bubbles in your champagne. It's also noticing your defensiveness after losing your temper, your helplessness in the face of injustice, or that the milk in your coffee has most definitely gone sour.

In short, mindfulness looks at the negative, the neutral, and the positive, all with equanimity. It's not joy—instead, it's the awareness of joy, but also of pain and everything else in between. It's taking a step back from the constant input of sensory information and the constant output of thoughts and feelings. Whether for a split second or many hours, it's your journey behind the waterfall.

Activity:
Think of a time or two that you could be consistently mindful each day. It could be when you eat your breakfast, or before you go to sleep at night.

Joyage #41: Shifting Perspective

"Change the way you see things, and the things you see will start to change" – Wayne Dyer

Many of the challenges of finding happiness stem from the problem of comparison. We find people or things that are better and compare our life to that life. Because of what we choose as our point of comparison, we often find ourselves lacking, and therefore focus on attaining some unachievable goal in the future; possibly berating ourselves for the mistakes we made in our past.

If we focus our point of comparison on growth in ourselves and on what we have, instead of what we don't have, we can truly start to appreciate the gift of the present. Are you happy to have a family member or friends? You could be completely alone in the world. Are you happy to have enough money to buy food? You could be going hungry every day. Are you happy to see the green trees and blue sky? They are beautiful parts of nature and should be appreciated because they may not always be within our sight. There can be pleasure in getting up every morning and preparing for a job. There can even be pleasure in getting up every morning and preparing to go look for a job. When you eat your breakfast, what aromas, tastes, and sensations do you experience? Take a moment to appreciate what is here and now. It is truly a gift only you get to experience in that moment.

It is a natural habit to compare ourselves to other people. But once we truly achieve a higher level of happiness, we can ignore those comparisons and focus on improving ourselves and our progress over time. For those of us not there yet, we can start by changing our point of comparison.

As a society we tend to group with people who are similar to us. We live and spend time with people who have the same nationality, similar income levels, similar values, similar education levels, similar interests, etc. When we start comparing ourselves, we look to the best in our comparison group. We compare ourselves to people who represent our aspirations, and because we tend only to see the aspirational parts of those people while we ignore the harsh or undiscovered realities, we never seem to match up and start to feel like we will never be good enough. This starts the cycle of focusing on the future and how we are going to work harder or do more to be prettier, richer, drive a nicer car, etc. If we ever feel we have finally reached that level; we stop and readjust only to find that there is yet another level to chase. We are constantly looking for the mythical "pot of gold at the end of the rainbow." And unfortunately, we usually never find the end of the rainbow.

One solution is to expand from a **mindset of comparison** to a **habit of mindfulness and gratitude**. What do we have right now that we can appreciate? There are millions of people around the world who are not as well off as we might be. We can focus on how our car is not as new or nice as our neighbor's car, or we can look at how many people don't have cars to drive at all. Our houses are not big enough or close enough to work, but we do have a place to live when millions don't. How about having running water and bathrooms? 3.2 billion people, or 43% of the world's population, do not have running water and bathrooms in their homes. Are you familiar with the phrase "Stop and smell the roses"? What is your commute like? Are you focused on how long or boring it is, or the never-ending traffic that appears? What if you chose to pause and appreciate the scenery along the way? The ponds, the architecture, the trees, the flowers. How about the people? There are interesting people getting off and on buses and trains - what makes them happy? What could you do to make them smile? How beautiful is the sky today? How refreshing is the rain? How exciting is the thunder and lightning?

"Sometimes we develop grand concepts of what happiness might look like for us, but if we pay attention, we can see that there are little symbols of happiness in every breath that we take." – His Holiness Gyalwang Karmapa

Activity:
On your way to and from work, practice mindfulness. Try to appreciate the scenery, or think about the other people on the road, and what jobs they may have or what joys they may have in their own lives.

Joyage #42: Why Is Mindfulness Beneficial?

"Yesterday is history. Tomorrow is a mystery. Today is a gift. That's why it is called the present." – Alice Morse Earle.

Mindfulness can help you choose the important over the urgent.

When we are children, before we become overwhelmed with the pressures of life or worrying about being as productive as possible, we are naturally mindful. When we see a toy or a friend, we stop what we were doing and put our full attention on playing. We don't evaluate or worry, we just start playing. We become completely absorbed in our games or our friends.

At some point however we learn the concept of scarcity, and we try to cram as much into our days as possible. We get so focused on finding productive hours that we forget to just "be" in those hours.

Our minds are good at categorizing. Everything we see or are exposed to gets categorized in our brain so we can quickly understand the world around us. At some point we start believing that since we have categorized it, we have all the information we need. Our natural curiosity wanes, and we see no need to gather more information. Since we think we know everything there is to know about the person or environment that is in front of us, we can get bored and start looking for something else that is more interesting.

Sometimes we get caught in a vicious cycle of quickly categorizing more and more new experiences, and therefore find fewer and fewer things to be excited about. Mindfulness is all about the process of stopping and discovering something more to be excited about. It requires us to realize that we really don't know everything there is to know about what we are eating, where we are walking, or even the person we are with. Re-igniting our curiosity gives us more opportunities to be happy as we find ways to re-engage with the world.

You can't wait to be happy in the future, because by definition the future never comes. To be happy, you must find ways to be happy today. Mindfulness is a great tool to make us aware of what is going on around us. If we are thinking about what we are doing and why we are doing it, we can monitor our behaviors and make adjustments.

In <u>Daring Greatly</u>, Brene Brown gave an example of eating chocolate: She asks if we are savoring the taste and texture of the chocolate and really enjoying the sensations, or are we just stuffing tons of chocolate in our mouths in an attempt to forget about some negative event or thought in our lives? We can use mindfulness as a tool to determine when we are savoring and should continue our activities, or when we are numbing and should probably stop to deal with our current feelings and challenges.

Activity:
Eat chocolate! Take one piece of chocolate and take a small bite. Notice the taste, the texture, and how it melts in your mouth. Is there anything new you've noticed while practicing mindfulness while you eat your chocolate? Continue to take small bites and practice mindfulness as you finish your piece of chocolate.

Closing Thoughts on Practicing Mindfulness:

To summarize what mindfulness is and is not:

1. Mindfulness is the ability to remove distractions and focus on what is happening right now, in this second.
2. Mindfulness is not meditation, taking time to relax, mindlessness, the ultimate goal, or always bliss.
3. In order to practice mindfulness, we'll need to shift our perspective
4. Mindfulness is good for us because it gives us an opportunity to be present over perfect.

How to Implement in Your Life

Do you want to make mindfulness a habit? Let's start with an easy one: Food. Try paying attention to everything you eat for the rest of the month. The taste, the texture, the consistency, aroma, flavor etc. Interesting tidbit - I did this and realized that Pringles weren't salted on both sides. (mind blown!)

Keep the following in mind to help you practice mindfulness:

Mindfulness is the ability to focus on what is truly important to you. The next time you catch yourself in a comparison trap, think of the present and what you can be grateful for in that moment. Appreciate what's around you to practice mindfulness.

Chapter 9: Developing Personally

"It is not because things are difficult that we do not dare; it is because we do not dare that they are difficult." – Lucius Annaeus Seneca

What You Will Learn in This Chapter:

1. How to conquer your fears.
2. How to recognize and overcome FOMO (Fear of Missing Out).
3. How to establish priorities and become more productive.

Introduction to Developing Personally

Personal Development refers to any activity that improves a person's talents, potential consciousness, or ideas to realize dreams or create wealth. In a nutshell, personal development is anything you do to become better. It's a process of self-education aimed at enhancing your values.

Six benefits of Personal Development are:
1. Self-awareness
2. Increased sense of direction
3. Clarity
4. Motivation
5. Resilience
6. Fulfilling relationships

Unfortunately, when it comes to personal development, there is no "one size fits all" approach. Each individual has a unique area they'd like to grow in, however one particular area rings true for many.

Fear is an issue we all deal with. Yet with this complicated emotion can come responses that vary drastically from one individual to the other. In this chapter, we'll learn particularly about the Fear Of Missing Out and why it's become more prevalent in our society. We'll also learn why it's not as absurd as it may sound, and how you can overcome and manage it.

Joyage #43: What Is the Psychology Behind FOMO?

"FOMO (fear of missing out) is the enemy of valuing your own time." –
Andrew Yang

Did you know that a closely related emotion to FOMO is Regret?

You might be thinking..."What does FOMO have to do with regret?"

Well, with FOMO, regret can be broadcast into the future, which is referred to as "affective forecasting"— trying to predict how we might feel based on events that haven't happened yet. We don't want to regret the fun we could've had.

To explain another way, in behavioral economics, and decision theory, the psychology behind FOMO can be partially explained by loss aversion. Amos Tversky and Daniel Kahneman demonstrated people's strong tendency to want to avoid any losses and the research suggests that losses are twice as impactful on people, psychologically, as gains. This leads to risk aversion; we just hate to lose out on anything.

The fear of missing out is an old—actually an ancient—fear, being triggered by the newest form of communication: social media.

Our survival as an individual within a tribe, and thus our survival as a species, once hinged on our being aware of threats both to ourselves and to the larger group. To be "in the know" when we roamed around in small groups was critical to survival. To not be aware of a new food source, for example, meant you literally missed out on something that could mean the difference between life and death.

When humans began to create more stable farming communities, being in the know involved paying attention, being in the right places at the right times to get resources and information, and engaging in the gossip of the day as it filtered through the community.

We all know that systems to consolidate and enhance communication among humans change. In order to keep each other informed of important information, including potential sources of danger to our tribes/countries/species, communication has developed over time and includes the forms we interact with today like television, newspapers, the Internet, and social media platforms.

Since regret causes us to pay attention and respond quickly, we actually have a part of our brain that is specialized for sensing if we are being left out. It's usually not a matter of life and death whether you are on Twitter or Instagram, but for many people social media has become their version of a community lifeline.

That specialized part of the brain, the amygdala, is a part of the limbic system, which detects whether something could be a threat to our survival. Not having vital information or getting the impression that one is not a part of the "in" group is enough for many individuals' amygdalas to engage the stress or activation response; otherwise known as the "fight or flight" response.

Feeling physically stressed does not feel good, and that is one of the reasons why people want to avoid feeling left out. They're trying to prevent the stress response!

But don't go too far in the other direction! Some of us redouble our efforts to not miss out on anything and end up in an almost constant process of "checking" behavior. That is, we're constantly looking at our Instagram or Twitter feeds to see if we're missing out on anything, which doesn't lessen our stress that much. Being in a hypervigilant state is the complete opposite of being at peace.

Activity:

Self-Evaluation/Inventory: For the rest of the day, track how many times you logged into social media. Then reflect on what other productive activities you could be doing with your time.

Joyage #44: What Type of Person Is Most Sensitive to FOMO?

"Focus on what makes you happy, and do what gives meaning to your life"
– Barry Schwartz

Social Media and our access to information has inundated us with a variety of different ways to feel left out, less than others, or simply not good enough. We are exposed to the extremes online, and "average" is unfortunately no longer an option. We sit day in and day out comparing our worst selves to others highlight reels and we are constantly left in a state of regret for what we didn't do instead of gratitude for what we did.

Dr. Barry Schwartz introduced a psychological principle behind FOMO called The Paradox of Choice.

The Principle explains that the more choices we have, the less happy we are with what we choose. Too many choices lead to anxiety and depressive FOMO feelings. The people most sensitive to FOMO, according to Schwartz, are maximizers, people who are always trying to get "the best" out of every situation.

Maximizers are more prone to regret, and depression over the choices they make, constantly wondering if it was the best choice. Their amygdalas are already highly sensitive to perceiving threats in the environment so they are already prone to over analyzing every part of their lives. This could include people who tend to be socially anxious, those who have experienced some kind of emotional trauma in the past, or people who tend to be obsessive or compulsive.

Activity:

Next time you have an important decision to make, work to eliminate as many options as possible prior to beginning your evaluation process. Rather than focusing on everything you might miss out on, focus on what you want to achieve or experience.

Joyage #45: Why Is FOMO Dangerous?

"Life is better when you do what makes you happy regardless of what others think. It's your life, not theirs." – Sonya Parker

Ever texted while driving? Ever respond to a text in the middle of a conversation with someone else? Do you carry your phone into meetings?

We've dumped ourselves into an era of instant gratification. It's easy to define our lives based on the virtual crowd who is watching, critiquing, and applauding our every move. It's even easier to conform to the crowd's mold -- constantly measuring our lives against a celebrity's Instagram post or a friend's life event.

This 'give me more' and 'I want that' attitude can be detrimental to us both physically and mentally. The problem with FOMO is that the individuals it impacts are looking outward instead of inward. When you're so tuned in to the 'other,' or the 'better' (in your mind), you lose your authentic sense of self. This constant fear of missing out means you are not participating as a real person in your own, real world.

According to Dr. Darlene McLaughlin, M.D., assistant professor at the Texas A&M Health Science Center College of Medicine, between three to thirteen percent of the population are diagnosed with a condition called social anxiety. She says that, "Part of social anxiety is the fear of being judged by others or embarrassing oneself in social interactions." The average young person spends eight to 10 hours killing time on their cell phone each day, and when we consistently believe we are 'missing out,' anxiety and depression may set in.

While we may not all experience severe social anxiety, sadly, many of us have pretty bad cases of FOMO -- even if we're unwilling to admit it. And, this incessant worrying about what everyone else is doing only causes us to miss out on our own lives even more.

So, what do we do? How do we overcome this?

Activity:
Think to yourself: Do you typically commit to an activity, or wait until the last minute to confirm plans? Why or why not? Do you ever feel anxious if you weren't included or invited to participate in an activity? Why or why not?

Joyage #46: How to Overcome FOMO? Meet #JOMO

"For everything you have missed, you have gained something else." –
Ralph Waldo Emerson

Alright. So, we've talked about the psychology behind FOMO, who's most sensitive to it, you were given an activity, and then told why FOMO could be bad for your health. Now, let's talk about how to beat it.

If you haven't heard this term, let us introduce you to the new trend: #JOMO: Joy Of Missing Out. – Sometimes missing out is a GREAT thing. JOMO is all about gratitude! And the good news is that countless research papers confirm this as a way to overcome FOMO.

A way to reduce FOMO and increase happiness is learning to accept "good enough."

Look around. What good things might you be taking for granted? Home? Family? Friends? Think about it. Now take a couple seconds to imagine those were taken away from you. How would you feel? Do you feel more grateful to have them? Mentally subtracting cherished moments from your life can help you appreciate them more, make you grateful, and ultimately, happier.

Another activity you can try comes from the Paradox of Choice we talked about earlier. Try reducing the number of options you consider before making a decision, and practice gratitude for what is good in a decision rather than focusing on regret and disappointments with what is less than ideal.

Are you seeing a theme here? Focusing on what is good about what we have physically changes the chemistry of our brains and the hormones that contribute to our feelings. The inevitable comparisons to the fake lives on social media makes you feel like you can never measure up to their standard.

Now, it's important to say that social media isn't the devil. But some of us are wired to compare ourselves to others, and you know where that leads on a medium where everyone is editing reality to look their best.

Social media can help you be happy. But don't scroll and compare. Use it to plan face-to-face get togethers. Columbia professor John Cacioppo, the leading researcher on loneliness, says even just doing that can make your life better. "Social Media is merely a tool," he says, "and like any tool, its effectiveness will depend on its user." If you use Facebook to increase face-to-face contact, it increases social capital. So if social media lets you organize a game of football among your friends, that's healthy. If you turn to social media instead of playing football, however, that's unhealthy.

And when you're with friends, put that phone away. Seeing friends and family regularly is the happiness equivalent of an extra $97,265 a year. Whatever you want to check on social media ain't worth a hundred grand...

Activity:
For the rest of the month, start and end each day with three things you're grateful for and would never want to lose. Then come back and journal about how it improved your life.

Joyage #47: Prioritizing - $100 Rocks

"People who can focus, get things done. People who can prioritize, get the right things done." – John Maeda

Our list of things to do always seems to be getting longer rather than shorter. In order to reach our goals, we want to make sure that we are focused on accomplishing the tasks most related to achievement of our goals. One method of prioritization is the $100 Rocks. As an analogy, picture two rooms. One is filled with rocks and the other is empty. Every day, in order to reach our goals, we have to move as many rocks as we can from the first room to the second room. Every rock has a value on it, from $1 to $100, which corresponds to the impact that rock will have on achieving our goals.

If we can only move five rocks a day, we want to make sure they are the rocks that most help us reach our goals. We can go into the first room and pick up two $5 rocks, two $25 rocks, and a $30 rock. Now at the end of the day we have moved five rocks and made $90 of progress toward our goals ($5 + $5 + $25 + $25 + $30 = $90). The other option is to pick out five $100 rocks. This time we have moved the same number of rocks and made $500 of progress toward our goals. The fastest way to reach our goals is to take a few extra minutes to pick out the $100 rocks. Once the $100 rocks are gone, we pick out the $99 rocks, and then the $98 rocks, etc.

Activity:
Prioritize Your List

1. Make a list of everything you have to do today. You can also do this for the week or the month.

2. Give everything a rock value based on how important it is to reaching your goals. For example, if your goal is to be healthier and that includes an exercise routine, then exercise would be a $90 rock while cleaning off your desk would be a $25 rock.

3. No rock values can be the same. You have to make a decision about each item relative to the other items on the list.

4. Start with the highest dollar rock and work your way down. You don't have to complete each task; you just have to make progress on it and know the next steps and timeframes before you start another task.

Joyage #48: Overcoming Your Fears

"You gain strength, courage and confidence by every experience in which you really stop to look fear in the face." – Eleanor Roosevelt

I want to tell you a story about when I was a young child (about 5 or 6). I was invited to a friend's house, and my friend's dad decided we should go to haunted house. I didn't know it at the time, but I hate haunted houses to this day. Paying to be terrorized is not my idea of fun. I remember two things about that night: first, I tried my best not to bust out in tears (mission failure) and second, I remember my little stubby fingers in the two side belt loops of that dad's jeans. I was walking right behind him holding onto him tightly with my head buried in my chest and my eyes closed as tight as they would go. I was terrified and pretty much ruined for life on haunted houses.

Thankfully, haunted houses only come around in October, but there are a lot of fears in our life. You may be bound by fear and it's keeping you from experiencing life the way you should. How do we handle fear when it becomes paralyzing?

I want to give you a couple of belt loops to hang onto.

First, you should determine what is causing the fear in your life. Are you fearful a relationship may go wrong? Or maybe you won't ever find that "right" person? Are you fearful you may lose your job and then not be able to find another one? Is it financial fears? Do you have fears about your physical health? Understanding what you truly believe to be the root of your fear can help you unpack the ways to tackle those anxieties.

Second, talk to someone about that fear. Whether it's a counselor, minister, or just a friend, sometimes their viewpoint can help you to put those fears into perspective and enable you to "get off your chest" what is making you afraid. Sometimes you need another person to remind you it's going to be ok and you will be alright if you don't let fear control you.

Finally, let your faith give you freedom over fear. No matter what belief system you embrace, often there are practices and beliefs that can help you overcome your fear. Memorizing scripture on fear, prayer, meditation, and even singing can reassure your heart and soul. Your faith can become an avenue of healing.

I may be the only one you know that doesn't like haunted houses, but nobody likes living in a constant state of fear. If you are being controlled by your fears, figure out what is causing the fear, talk it out with someone, then let your faith help you to overcome what has you frightened.

Activity:
Take a minute to determine what is causing the fear in your life. Are you fearful a relationship may go wrong? Or maybe you won't ever find that "right" person? Are you fearful you may lose your job and then not be able to find another one? Is it financial fears? Do you have fears about your physical health? Schedule a time this week to talk to someone about that fear.

Closing Thoughts on Developing Personally

"The two most important days in your life are the day you are born and the day you find out why." – Mark Twain

Is your brain on overload? Do you need a quick summary? Ok, here it is:

Fear of Missing Out starts with sadness. Conquer you fears by recognizing what causes them, talking to someone about your fear, and then let your faith give you freedom over your fear.

Social media makes it worse, not better. Facebook isn't evil – but relying on it for happiness is. Remember to not compare your worst to their best. Recognize your FOMO if you find yourself scrolling on social media looking for happiness. Instead of comparing yourself to people on the internet, create a gratitude journal and write three things every day that you are grateful for.

Managing priorities can be hard, using $100 Rocks can make it easier where you should start and what should come next on your list.

Finally, don't let your fears hold you back. They are a natural part of your life and we all have them. Identify what you fear most. Reach out to a friend and talk about. Learn to conquer your fears and your potential is unlimited.

Chapter 10: Creating Habits

"Habit is a cable; we weave a thread of it each day, and at last we cannot break it." – Horace Mann

What You'll Learn in This Chapter:
1. Habits have the power to change your life for the better.
2. How to identify the cue, routine, and reward of a habit.
3. How to create, modify, and build off good habits to help you achieve your goals.

Introduction to Creating Habits

"We first make our habits, and then our habits make us." – John Dryden

You are a creature of habit. You brush your teeth every night out of habit. Every morning, you drive to work without much thought, because it's a habit. You make coffee, sweep the floor, fill out spreadsheets, walk the dog, watch TV, and take out the trash without needing to concentrate, because all these actions are habits.

Habits are automatic behaviors that are triggered by cues in your environment. Habits make up about 45% of your daily actions, and for some types of tasks, this percentage is much higher!

Three researchers named Wood, Quinn, and Kashy had 70 people track their thoughts, feelings, and actions every hour.

They found that habits make up around:

- 88% of hygiene-related behaviors
- 81% percent of sleeping and waking behaviors
- 58% of traveling-related behaviors
- 55% of job-related tasks, and
- 54% of leisure and entertainment choices

It's crazy to realize how much of life is performed completely out of habit. This is both a good and a bad thing, depending on how you look at it. On the one hand, it's easy for bad habits to overtake your life. On the other hand, once you learn how habits work, you can use them to your advantage.

In this Joyage on habits, you will learn how to create good habits, modify bad habits, follow through on your intentions, form habit chains, and use habits to reach your goals. Don't be fooled into thinking that habits are too ordinary to make a difference. Used in the right way, habits have the power to change your life.

Joyage #49: Habits Are Powerful Tools

"We are what we repeatedly do. Excellence then, is not an act but a habit."
– Will Durant

Ok, wait a minute. Are habits really life-changing? Maybe the promise of life-changing results sounds too good to be true. Are habits really that powerful?

One of the first people to describe the power and purpose of habits was the psychologist William James. In his book, The Principles of Psychology, first published in 1890, James said this about habits: "The more of the details of our daily life we can hand over to the effortless custody of automatism, the more our higher powers of mind will be set free for their own proper work." In other words, habits allow you to complete daily actions without effort, which provides extra cognitive space to focus on more important, goal-directed work.

James goes on to say that habits are powerful because they turn the nervous system into an "ally." James understood that habits become hardwired into your brain. When you complete a task over and over again, your nervous system begins to remember the task for you, which eventually allows you to complete the task without thought.

When you turn daily actions into effortless habits, you feel less stressed and more in control. You save up discipline for other areas of life, which allows you to accomplish more each day. When you are strategic about the type of habits you add to your life, they serve as powerful tools that can help you reach your goals.

Before moving forward with the course, think of one long-term goal you want to accomplish and take a moment to write it down. Keep this goal in mind as you learn about habits. Think of it as the destination you want your habits to take you. It's the reason creating habits is worth it in the first place.

Activity:
Write down one long term goal you wish to achieve.

Joyage #50: The Anatomy of a Great Habit

"Good habits are the key to all success. Bad habits are the unlocked door to failure." – Og Mandino

To create habits that lead you towards your goals, you need to understand how habits are formed. Habits follow recognizable patterns composed of several parts. Taken together, these parts form a habit loop.

One version of the habit loop is described by Charles Duhigg in his book The Power of Habit. According to Duhigg, habits are composed of a cue, a routine, and a reward.

A cue is something in the environment that triggers the habit such as a time of day, an emotional state, a place, a person, or a preceding action. The cue triggers the routine, which is the behavior that makes up the habit. Finally, the reward is the metaphorical prize you get for completing the habit, which encourages you to return to the behavior.

For example, John has a habit of eating cookies every night. When he has finally finished helping his kids settle into bed, this is his cue to walk downstairs, head to the kitchen, and open the cookie tin. The routine is eating the cookies, and the reward is the delicious taste.

Think of a habit in your life and identify the cue, routine, and reward. Once you learn to identify each part of a habit, you can control your habits in a number of different ways. For example, you can....

- Influence cues in your life to break a habit or initiate a new one.
- Set goals that determine the type of routine you want to remove, create, or replace.
- Add or remove rewards to encourage or discourage different habits.

As you can see, there are so many ways to use habits to lead you toward your goals!

Activity:
Think of a habit you have and identify the cue, routine, and reward.

Joyage #51: Create Good Habits

"A bad habit never disappears miraculously. It's an undo-it-yourself project" – Abigail Van Buren

Let's take a closer look at how good habits are created. Researchers Lally, van Jaarsvel, Potts and Wardle conducted a study in which participants set a goal to add one new health behavior that they would complete in the same context every day. The context was the cue. The goal was the routine. And the researchers decided not to add any external rewards such as money or other incentives. They then tracked how long it took for each participant's goal to become a habit. Here is what they found:

The more consistently participants repeated a behavior in the same context, the faster it became automated. On average, it took two months for a health behavior to become automatic. However, this number ranged from 18-254 days, depending on the participant. Although repetition was key to habit formation, a single missed opportunity didn't prevent participants from forming habits. The lack of external reward didn't prevent habit formation, either, which indicated that choosing behaviors you want to perform can be naturally rewarding.

Activity:
You can use this information to help you create a habit of your own:

1. Identify a behavior that will take you one step closer to your long-term goal.

2. Identify how you can perform that behavior in the same context every day.

3. Identify what makes the behavior naturally rewarding. (You can also consider adding an external reward, such as the promise of a new outfit once you reach your weight goal).

4. Commit to sticking with the behavior for at least 30 days.

5. If you miss a day, don't get discouraged. Just pick right back up where you left off.

Use these five steps to create a plan right now. Write your plan down and get started on it today.

Joyage #52: Modify Bad Habits

"I fear not the man who has practiced 10,000 kicks, but I do fear the man who has practiced one kick 10,000 times." – Bruce Lee

Everyone struggles with bad habits: Nail-biting. Over-eating. Cigarettes. Too much TV, social media, or shopping.

Bill is no exception. Every morning on his way to work, Bill stops and buys an extra-large mocha latte with whipped cream and chocolate syrup. If he doesn't modify this habit, he will never reach his goal weight. What should he do?

To start, Bill identifies each part of his habit loop – the cue, routine, and reward. Once he does, he experiments with several strategies.

Strategy #1: Avoid or remove the cue. Bill is cued to buy a latte when he passes by his favorite coffee shop on the way to work. Bill avoids the cue by taking a different route each morning. When he doesn't pass by the coffee shop, he isn't triggered to stop and buy a latte.

Strategy #2: Replace the routine. When Bill passes by the coffee shop, he lets that cue him to stop and buy a healthy green tea or smoothie instead of his normal latte.

Strategy #3: Identify and replace the reward. Bill considers how his daily coffee drink rewards him. He realizes he feels exhausted every morning, which leads him to crave caffeine and sugar. He brainstorms how he can find this reward elsewhere and decides to start working out in the morning before his commute. Working out rewards him with the same burst of energy as caffeine, which helps him no longer crave his daily lattes, and has the added benefit of helping him reach his goal of losing weight.

Activity:

Identify one habit that is getting in the way of your long-term goal. Then do some investigating. What is the cue and how can you avoid it? What is the routine and how can you replace it? What is the reward, and how can you find that reward elsewhere?

Joyage #53: Follow Through

"It is the follow through that makes the great difference between ultimate success and failure." – Charles Kettering

It takes from 30 to 90 days for a behavior to turn into a habit. This poses a dilemma: How do you stick with a behavior while you wait for it become automatic?

Consider three possible ways:

You can start by writing down a 'where and when' statement. Research by Milne, Orbell, and Sheeran compared two groups of people who both had intentions to exercise. One group wrote down where and when they planned to exercise. The other group did not. Ninety-one percent of the individuals who wrote down a where and when statement followed through with exercising, as opposed to only 38% of individuals who did not write out a statement.

Another strategy recommended by James Clear in his book, Atomic Habits, is habit tracking. According to Clear, tracking habits is beneficial because it is motivating, satisfying, and functions as a visual reminder to follow through.

There are many ways to track habits including using a calendar to mark the days you follow through, keeping a habit journal, or adding a coin or paperclip to a jar, every time you complete the habit.

Finally, tell someone about the habit you want to develop, ask that person to keep you accountable, and update that person with your progress on a regular basis.

It takes effort and planning, but it's possible to follow through with actions until they become habits. All your hard work will be worth it in the end!

Activity:
Do one, two, or all the following to follow through on your habit.

1. Create an if-then plan for your bad-habit modification and write it down. For example, "If I am still tired after my morning workout, then I will treat myself to a nutritious smoothie instead of a mocha latte."

2. Keep track every day this month if you follow through on a calendar or in a habit journal.

3. Find someone today to keep you accountable on following through. Update them regularly on your progress

Joyage #54: Form Habit Chains

"A keystone habit leads to other positive habits and disciplines. These positive traits start a chain reaction that produces other positive outcomes." – Craig Groeschel

Now that you know how to follow through on individual habits, the next step is to create a series of habits that will lead you towards your long-term goal. A great way to do this is to identify a keystone habit and use it to form a habit chain.

Keystone habits were first described by Duhigg in his book, <u>The Power of Habit</u>. Keystone habits are powerful behaviors that initiate a positive chain reaction that impacts your whole life. Exercise is one common keystone habit – many people find that daily exercise helps them want to eat better, sleep better, and live a more positive life.

For example, Kelly's long-term goal is to become a yoga instructor. The most important habit Kelly needs to focus on is practicing yoga, so she makes this her keystone habit. Every morning she wakes up at 6:00AM and begins her yoga routine.

Kelly uses her yoga practice to initiate the beginning of a habit chain. Habit chains are created when the routine of one habit becomes the cue of a second habit. Kelly starts her habit chain by using the end of her daily yoga practice as a cue to begin meditating.

Over the next few months, she adds more habits to her chain until it looks like this: yoga practice → meditation → reading yoga manual → smoothie for breakfast. The routine of each habit functions as the cue for the next habit, until she finds herself staying productive all morning without much thought.

What keystone habit can help you reach your goals? How can that keystone habit form the beginning of a habit chain that will give you effortless self-control over your daily routine?

Activity:
Choose a goal and identify a keystone habit that will help you reach your goal. Then, practice that habit for thirty days in a row. Once it becomes a habit, add a second habit. Repeat this process each month for a year to help you reach your goal.

Closing Thoughts on Creating Habits

"How we spend our days is of course, how we spend our lives. What we do with this hour, and that one, is what we are doing." – Annie Dillard

Dillard makes a compelling point. She reminds us that changing your life requires changing how you spend your hours and your days. And, as you already know, the best way to change your hours and days is to change your habits.

Most lives are not transformed in one miraculous moment, but through a series of small changes that accumulate over time. James Clear describes this process in his book, Atomic Habits. He tells the story of a man named Dave Brailsford who was hired as the performance director of the British cycling team at a time when the team was struggling.

Brailsford set out to transform the team through a concept called "the aggregation of marginal gains." He made hundreds of tiny improvements in all areas of the team's performance. He adjusted bike seats, tires, and uniform material. He changed their pillows, mattresses, massage gels, and workouts. All these marginal improvements added up to something amazing. Under Brailsford's leadership, Britain shot out of mediocrity and went on to set records and win medals at the Olympic games, Tour de France, and the World Championships.

Don't be discouraged by humble beginnings. Start with one habit, and work on it until it becomes automatic. Know your final goal and work towards marginal gains in all areas of life that support that goal. Change your habits, and you will eventually change your life.

How to Implement in Your Life

Pick something you want to change to be happier, like being on a diet, getting more organized, spending less money, or just finding ways to enjoy life. Then, schedule 15 minutes every day, preferably in the morning when your willpower is full, and spend that time working on your new habit.

Next, print out a paper calendar with 30 days on it. Every morning when you complete your new habit-forming task, mark an X on the calendar. Keep the calendar in a prominent place where you can see it. Try to mark an X on each day and aim not to miss more than two days in a row.

Conclusion

Keep the following in mind to help you form habits:

A large majority of your life is made up of habits. Use this to your advantage to save discipline for other areas of your life that you would like to improve.

After identifying the cue, routine, and reward for your habit, consider the following ways to change your habit into a positive one:

a. Influence cues in your life to break a habit or initiate a new one.
b. Set goals that determine the type of routine you want to remove, create, or replace.
c. Add or remove rewards to encourage or discourage different habits.

Create a plan to build a new habit in your life. Identify what behavior will help you reach your goal, how you can do it every day, and a reward for performing the behavior. Commit to doing it every day and tell a friend about it for accountability. After successfully building your new habit, add another habit to begin forming a habit chain.

"We are what we repeatedly do. Excellence is not an act, but a habit." – Will Durant

Pick your favorite concept from this chapter and share with a friend!

Conclusion

Thank You for spending your valuable time learning a few Joyages. Don't forget to download the app to learn even more and to help you practice the skills you have learned.

Happiness isn't all cotton candy and rainbows. We're conditioned by social media, family, and friends to think that we need to be happy all the time. They all make it seem that being unhappy means something is wrong in your life. Joyages is here to help you change your mindset around happiness and to let you know that it's okay to be unhappy, because you can get back to being happy with the right skills and habits.

We workout to get stronger, we eat healthier to prevent disease, we brush our teeth twice a day to prevent cavities. We do so many things to maintain our health, but often neglect to train our brain to handle life's inevitable challenges. We have created Joyages, the book and the app, to help you brush your brain and improve your Brain Health. This book has hopefully helped you get back to your happy by teaching you how to handle life's toughest moments through three-minute lessons and habit recommendations. Don't spend your life trying to be happy all the time, learn how to prepare to handle and prevent the challenges you will face.

Please reach out to us at: Info@Joyages.com.

If you enjoyed Joyages: 3 Minutes to Emotional Health, please leave us a positive review on Amazon.

About Joyages

 Joyages is devoted to solving the mental health crisis in America. Joyages launched in 2019, but is built on decades of clinical research presented in a smartphone-enabled environment that is highly engaging and follows best practices in adult learning theory. Joyages exists because too much of mental healthcare is focused on helping people post-crisis. Instead, we asked a simple question: What if we could help prevent the crisis?

Download the Joyages app today.

Made in the USA
Monee, IL
23 September 2020

42747897R00098